Teacher Under Construction: Things I Wish I'd Known!

Teacher Under Construction: Things I Wish I'd Known!

A Survival Handbook for New Middle School Teachers

Eight Critical Building Blocks for Success Every New Middle School Teacher Should Know the First Year

Jerry L. Parks, Ed.S., NBCT

Weekly Reader Press
New York Lincoln Shanghai

Teacher Under Construction: Things I Wish I'd Known!
A Survival Handbook for New Middle School Teachers

Weekly Reader Press
an imprint of iUniverse, Inc.
and the Weekly Reader Corporation

For information address:
iUniverse, Inc.
2021 Pine Lake Road, Suite 100
Lincoln, NE 68512
www.iuniverse.com

ISBN: 0-595-33094-0

Printed in the United States of America

Contents

1. Professionalism: *Building a Teacher—*

Principle—"The first step in becoming a professional is *presenting* yourself as one!"

Lesson I must learn: Your professionalism will be seen in everything you do and say within your classroom. Be sure you take your professionalism seriously. The impressions you make on other teachers, parents, and students will be lasting ones. Make them positive!

2. Structure: *Building a Classroom—*

Principle—"A good teacher teaches *students* the subject, not the *subject* to students!"

Lesson I must learn: The more efficiently your classroom learning environment functions, the greater success you will have in promoting student achievement. Create a classroom where your students *want* to learn and *enjoy* coming to class. If you can do this, you will smooth the road to successful learning!

3. Support: *Building Parental Resources—*

Principle—"Your most valuable resource is the one you will most seldom use!"

Lesson I must learn: The parents of your students are an invaluable resource. Utilize and appreciate them at every opportunity, and you will gain the most important ally you will ever have as a teacher!

4. Maintenance: *Building Relationships—*

Principle—"Everything you needed to know to become a teacher—they *didn't* teach you at the university!"

Lesson I must learn: 'Big doors often swing on small hinges.' There are small but important things you must remember in order to become a successful teacher, and the way you deal with your staff, duties, and personal responsibilities will determine your success or failure as a teacher. Learn these lessons well!

5. **Content:** *Building a Lesson—*
the bricks and mortar of learning!..**30**

Principle—"An ounce of need will go further than a pound of content!"

Lesson I must learn: Your familiarity with the subject you teach—and the way you present the information—is the heart and soul of your job. Know your content, and distribute it in a way that is easily digestible to the children you teach!

6. **Attitudes:** *Building Atmosphere—*
creating a magical environment!..**40**

Principle—"As a teacher, your job is not to fill a bucket, but to light a fire!"

Lesson I must learn: Your attitude toward your subject and your students is the most important key to student achievement. Your students will often learn more from the fire of your presentation than from the information in your lesson. Be excited! Enjoy what you do!

Preface

"The entrance to the student's mind is through the child's heart."

Jessica ran into my room one morning, bubbling with excitement! "Come see my locker!" she urged, while spilling a half dozen gummy bears upon my recently organized desk. "I've decorated!"

Obligingly, I followed the precocious twelve-year-old into the hall. As she opened her locker for me to behold, Jessica beamed with pride. An unremarkable metal-encased hole in a wall had now been wonderfully transformed into the home away from home for her belongings for the next 180 days. As I marveled at Jessica's masterpiece of décor, I glimpsed, on the inside of her locker door, a photograph of the cutest collection of puppies I had ever seen. 'So typical,' I thought to myself, 'of what would win the heart of a little girl. How cute!'

Suddenly, my eyes glanced to the interior of Jessica's locker. Lovingly taped to the back wall was the full-body pin-up of the latest teen idol, scantily clad, and enticing in appearance. It was then that it hit me—*this* is what a middle schooler is! Random motion, jumbled chaos, and predictable unpredictability—a child becoming an adult—paused for one magical moment between puppies and sex symbols, and running on hormones and gum, with engines that somehow seem to never run out of gas.

As a new middle school teacher, you are about to embark upon the most wonderful and challenging career you could ever have chosen! You will have the experience of watching the birth and maturity of individualism, as sixth graders—like precocious nestlings—emerge from the shell of childhood. You will marvel at the diversity of personality development, as seventh graders test their wings of adolescent freedom—and your patience—with emergent maturity. Finally, you will beam with pride in watching eighth graders take flight into high school—talents and skills now better identified—in no small part because of you.

You will be told often that teaching middle school is the most difficult teaching assignment of all. Perhaps it is. But if you are willing to put in the hard work that teaching this age-level requires, you will find working with middle schoolers the most rewarding daily experience on planet Earth! *"Teacher Under Construction: Things I Wish I'd Known!"* is merely an effort to get you started off on the right foot.

If an expert is an ordinary person who attempts extraordinary feats, then I qualify. Not because this book presents concepts that are new or profound, but because for *any* individual to presume to have empirically correct answers as to what makes the perfect middle teacher is as *extraordinary* as it is *impossible*.

This book is not intended to be a compendium of teaching strategies, research, or procedures. There are many books available for these. *"Teacher Under Construction: Things I Wish I'd Known!"* is only intended to be a ready-reference basic training manual to equip newer middle school teachers with enough information to survive the first year of middle school. It is merely a jump-start guide to support the novice instructor until he or she can formulate personal paradigms of what works and what doesn't. Much of the information will be relevant across the curriculum. Other information is gleaned from twenty years of personal experience in the social studies classroom. All of the information is suitable to personal adaptation, and is presented in light of pragmatic practicality rather than exhaustive research.

It is said that 'teachers are born with the talent, but *good* teachers are made by the experience.' One purpose of this book is to allow talented teachers to *become* good teachers. Research tells us that less than 60% of new teachers will remain in the classroom after five years. Only in seeing the profession as a satisfying and enjoyable environment can talented teachers develop the experiences that make a successful middle school teacher. Experienced teachers, on the other hand, may recognize within these pages much of what they already do, for time has a way of quickly refining, for every teacher, what will and won't work in a middle school classroom.

The information and suggestions found within these pages are the culmination of many years of presenting at conferences across the country, including regular sessions at the *National Middle School Association* national convention. They reflect my personal philosophy in dealing with middle schoolers. Although most have been validated by research, they are not intended to be paradigms of the latest and greatest methodology in our field.

It is hoped that all teachers will be able to utilize, refine, and modify the information presented in this book, and in doing so, avoid many of the pitfalls that line the paths of inexperience in the middle school classroom. The suggestions and teaching strategies do not work because I offer them. I offer them because they work.

I would like to thank the thousands of teenagers who have surrendered one year of their lives to be my students at *Tates Creek Middle School* in Lexington, KY, and *Georgetown Middle School*, in Georgetown, KY. Without their patience, and the support of innumerable professional peers with whom I've had the pleasure to work, this book would not have been possible.

Jerry L. Parks, NBCT
Georgetown Middle School
Email: *Kidztchr7@hotmail.com*

What is a Middle Schooler?

By J.L.Parks

A middle schooler is random motion, jumbled chaos, and predictable unpredictability—a child becoming an adult—paused for one magical moment between pictures of puppies, and pin-ups of sex symbols. They are a walking paradox of fashionless style, fueled by hormones and gum, and fired by engines that seem to never run out of gas. They are strongly independent social creatures that travel in packs and communicate by sacred note. They are nourished by the immediate, unencumbered by past, and impatient for the tomorrow they feel will never come.

Middle schoolers can miss the obvious, harp on the obscure, and defend the impossible. They thrive on spontaneity, loathe predictability, and refuse to even acknowledge the parents they love. They deny the proven, dispute the certain, stand up for the irrelevant, and fall out of chairs. Tapping is their anthem, and fairness—their rule of life. They are possessed of selective memory, and a fierce loyalty to their own kind. Their hair is their banner, disorder—their creed. Their image is the only thing that matters more than lunch.

Middle schoolers are bolts of energy wrapped in a package of laziness. They are confusion poured into mood swings—fueled by encouragement, motivated by curiosity, and stimulated by challenge. They are inspired by sincerity, frustrated by denial, and defeated by doubt. They are gangly growth spurts with a twinkle in their eyes. They are confident pretenders masquerading in fragile shells of insecurity—trusting skeptics—secretly searching for heroes.

Middle schoolers love to be hugged, but hate to be touched. They are reactive agents who cling to routine while reaching for change. They are reminders of our own immortality; in-progress paradigms of possibility in whose lives we plant a lesson, shape a behavior, mold a character, and seal a destiny. They are the first blooms of tomorrow's hope—fleeting sunbeams of a thirteenth springtime—on loan to a winter world.

1. Professionalism: *Building a Teacher— finding the professional within you!*

Principle—"The first step in becoming a professional is *presenting* yourself as one!"

Lesson I must learn: Your professionalism will be seen in everything you do and say within your classroom. Be sure you take your professionalism seriously. The impressions you make on other teachers, parents, and students will be lasting ones. Make them positive!

> ➤ Appearances are everything!
> ➤ The *'attitude challenge!'*
> ➤ The Nike Factor: 'Growing Pro!'
> ➤ The lesson from the cow!
> ➤ Your most important Latin lesson!

Appearances are everything!

When I spent time selling real estate, one of the first things I was told was the importance of my attire. Dressing nicely served a twofold purpose. First, it created a professional appearance for those with whom I dealt. Second, it made me *feel* professional, and made it easier for me to perform as one.

As a teacher, it may not be practical to wear a coat and tie or dress clothing to school. Neither is it professional to dress like the students you will teach. Strive to achieve the happy medium. Unless your school has a dress code for teachers, dress comfortably enough to do your job effectively, yet nicely enough to be seen as the professional you are. (Comfortable shoes are *especially* important.) Make no mistake—the way you dress in your classroom affects the respect your students will have for you, and the authority they perceive you to possess. The professional world has long known that we perform more effectively if we dress more professionally. Balance comfort

1

and appearance. Never forget, however, you are *not* the age of your students. Don't try to dress like them.

Your personal appearance is only part of your professionalism. The appearance of your room, grade book, and planning book also tells a story. Keep your classroom looking as though your students were coming in—not as though they had already been there. Balance a creative and exciting classroom appearance with a clean and inviting atmosphere. Keep your grade book organized. Write out lesson plans, and keep your planning book such that the substitute can read and understand it. Days will come when they will need to.

While all aspects of how you present yourself are vital, the most important part of your appearance is your vocabulary. Not only your students, but also the peers and parents you work with every day, will evaluate you by the words that come out of your mouth. You are a communicator by profession—learn how to speak correctly. If you can't speak with a teacher's authority, you will have difficulty inspiring confidence in your students and your peers.

Many years ago, I attended a national conference for educators and looked forward to a session led by one of the premier writers in the field. I went to the session early, and, because so many others were excited to hear this presenter, I found it difficult to find a seat. Squeezed in on the back row, I waited—pen in hand—for the pearls of wisdom I was sure would make me a better teacher. The speaker began by offering helpful information on classroom management, but as he continued, I noticed how often he managed to butcher the English language. Soon, I found myself noting the speaker's language and diction rather than his content. Not only was it unpleasant to listen to, but the poor diction and improperly spoken English reduced the confidence I had in the speaker.

Excelling as a public speaker is not a prerequisite for being a good teacher. Using correct diction (and *spelling!*), however, and correctly mastering the English language is! You *will* make an impression—one way or another—by the vocabulary that comes out of your mouth. Even if you cannot speak *professionally*, learn to speak *correctly*. Your students who must listen to you deserve no less. The way you speak not only creates an appearance, it inspires confidence.

There is one lesson you teach every day to every student. That lesson is modeling.

The way you allow your students to speak to you also affects your professionalism. Never allow them to call you by your first name, or simply by your last name alone. Insist that they be respectful enough to address you with 'Mr.', 'Ms.', 'Mrs.', or 'Dr.' You've been where they are, but they've never been in your position. Demand respect.

Finally, it should go without saying that the subject of your conversations at school should always be appropriate for the environment in which you work. While the kids may think you're cool by adopting their language, or laughing at questionable jokes, remember, *you* are the professional. You will gain no lasting respect by talking like your students. Be careful what you say around them. Be an *example* of what you'd like them to be—not a *buddy* who speaks their lingo. Never forget, you are always being evaluated by the words that come out of your mouth. You are a professional—act like one.

The 'Attitude Challenge!'

There are three very contagious entities in a middle school classroom: boredom, apathy, and enthusiasm. Propagate the last, and the first two will cease to exist. *Attitude*, that is, how you feel about your subject and job, *creates* atmosphere. If your students know you love what you do, and genuinely care about them, you will create an atmosphere where learning takes place. In middle school, the old maxim is never truer: students don't care how much you know until they know how much you care—about them, about your subject, about your job.

> Remember the '*Law of Teaching Triangulation*': If you care about your students, and you care about your subject, you can get your students to care about your subject!

Here is a challenge I often make to new teachers. I have yet to have one tell me it doesn't work. Show your students you love your subject, make them feel you also love them, and your students will love your class!

The Nike factor: 'Growing Pro!'

Nike was the Greek goddess of victory. In recent commercials, the Nike Company employed a catchphrase, '*Just do it!*' Such an edict is sometimes required for us as teachers because of our reticence to perform activities that seem to reside just outside the realm of importance. Such activities are important, however, and will make you more familiar with your subject, enable you to create more effective lesson plans, and improve your standing in the education profession. Considering these as priorities right now may not seem as important as teaching your students, but as Nike says—*just do it!*

First, join your state and national associations. It's good policy as a teaching professional. These organizations can offer you legal assistance, liability insurance, and professional development opportunities, as well as helpful publications and discounts.

Second, attend—and consider presenting at—*NMSA* and your subject area conferences. You can do this solo or as part of your team. Conferencing is the one single most effective professional development you can do. Let me repeat—*this is the one single most effective professional development you can do.* In attending these, you are learning from your peers—teachers just like you. You will return with innovative and successfully proven teaching ideas, become aware of the latest strategies and research in your field, and be able to share information with others who can learn from *you.* Apply and check funds early—these conferences are highlights of the school year.

Third, read the literature in your field. Subscribe to a journal. Be aware of the latest research. Learn how to utilize the Educational Research Information Center (ERIC). Grow *better* in what you do—don't just grow older.

Fourth, learn how to network. Get 'in the loop' or 'on the grapevine' of what's taking place in education. Join or organize a support group. Volunteer for county and state committees involving curriculum, textbooks, and testing. Communicate with others in your field. Learn from them. Allow them to learn from you. Join teacher chat rooms on the Internet, and keep abreast of what others in your subject area are doing that really *works.*

Fifth, present yourself as a professional. Create a business card to pass out at conferences, or wherever you may want to let other professionals know you are proud to be an educator! Cards can be designed online inexpensively, and should reflect you as a teacher. Be creative! Include a short but memorable quote, or personal philosophy of teaching. Don't forget to include your school email. A business card makes you look professional and comes in handy at conferences and parent meetings.

Sixth, keep an ongoing personal portfolio. You are growing as a professional, and should document your accomplishments along the way. Keep letters from parents and the community, as well as touching notes from students. (See Appendix: *Important documents to keep!*) Keep an updated resume. Catalogue your evaluations and professional development. These will come in handy when you least expect it, and prove invaluable should you seek *National Board Certification* in the future.

Seventh, recognize your limits. Learn how to say *no* sometimes—you can't do everything. For example, don't attempt to sponsor clubs and organizations until you become comfortable with your role as teacher. Don't frustrate yourself trying to accomplish the impossible. Set goals, but set *realistic* goals. Learn to prioritize. Conserve your energy. Find a hobby. Recognize that there is no shame in putting aside the business of school for a while.

Eighth, whether in an official or unofficial capacity, seek out and learn from a mentor. Experienced teachers have much to offer and can share advice that will save you time, frustration, and difficulty in every aspect of your job as teacher. Such teachers will not seek you out. Find them, sit in on their classes and take notes—pick their brains, and do not perceive them as professionals from a bygone era. Really listen to them. *Do not copy them*, but understand their wisdom will make you a better teacher.

Finally, never make big—possibly life-changing—decisions your first year of teaching. This is a stressful and challenging time at best, and not the time to make career choices you might possibly regret later. Realize that your first years are the most difficult of all, and that big decisions are better made when you are settled into a career rather than when you are simply trying to establish one.

The lesson from the cow!

I once heard a story about an old country preacher who got all his sermon material from the sermons of other preachers. He was often seen copying sermon illustrations from radio ministers and carefully noting various tidbits from every evangelist that came to his city. Finally, one of his parishioners approached him to ask why he thought it necessary to copy every other minister's material instead of coming up with his own. *"Why, it's a lesson I learned from my cow"*, the preacher responded. *"She grazes on many pastures, but she gives her own milk."*

Learn from many sources, and modify their ideas to suit your own style. Watch experienced teachers—sit in on their classes during a planning period. Consider suggestions and recommendations on your evaluations. Read the latest research. When you have seen what others do or recommend, modify it to your teaching style, your students, and subject area—and see if it works.

Your most important Latin lesson!

A final way that you exhibit professionalism is in your relationship to your students, and this is the most important relationship of all.

In loco parentis. The most important Latin lesson you, as a professional educator, will ever learn. *In loco parentis*—'in the position or place of a parent.' This is your legal status regarding the lives entrusted to your care, and you'd better never—*ever*—forget it.

As a teacher, you are held legally responsible for every word you say and every action you take regarding the children you teach. You are expected to know what is—and is not—appropriate in a public school classroom. This is more than just an important responsibility—it's the law. Ignorance is no excuse. You'd better take special care what you say or do regarding your students. Think long and hard before you tell that crude or questionable joke. Remember your audience.

Do not allow yourself to compromise—or be compromised—in your status as a professional educator. For example, never—*ever,* show inappropriate films in your classroom. If there is a question at all regarding videos, have an administrator preview them with you, and/or send home a permission slip.

Also, think carefully before you take a student home in your car, put your hands on a student, or allow yourself to be alone for an extended period with a student of the opposite sex. Consider carefully what books you assign for reading, what pictures you show, and—above all—what language you use in front of impressionable middle schoolers. Countless careers have been clouded by one unwise choice made in a school classroom. Innumerable reputations have been ruined by teachers who allowed themselves to be put into a compromising situation. *You are establishing a reputation with students and their families that will follow you for many years. Do not damage it with unwise actions.* What students may initially think makes you 'cool' can eventually damage your reputation and will never earn you lasting respect as a teacher. Regarding what you say or do around your students, a good rule of thumb to remember is: when in doubt—*don't.*

In loco parentis. The most important Latin lesson you will ever learn.

The least I need to know: My to do checklist!

- ❑ I will remember that I will *first* be judged by my appearance, and by my abilities afterward.
- ❑ I will not strive to dress like my students. I will balance professional dress with comfort.
- ❑ I will remember that after my appearance, the next things I will be judged by are the words that come out of my mouth.
- ❑ I will remember to insist that my students address me by name in a respectful manner.

- ❏ I will remember that organization is paramount, and there is a direct relationship between organization and effectiveness as a teacher.
- ❏ I will remember that students generally rise to the level of expectation set for them.
- ❏ I will remember that the three most contagious entities in middle school are boredom, apathy, and enthusiasm.
- ❏ I will remember that my students don't care how much I know until they know how much I care—about them, and my job.
- ❏ I will remember that I am a professional, and a lifelong learner, and that learning began—not ended—with my hire.
- ❏ I will get involved with professional organizations and committees within my school system and the state.
- ❏ I will seek out a mentor, and keep and update a personal portfolio.
- ❏ I will make sure I have a life outside of school with hobbies, interests and friends.
- ❏ I will attend meetings and conferences for my subject area as often as I am able.
- ❏ I will learn from others, and modify to suit my students and subject area.
- ❏ I will *never* allow myself to be put in compromising situations with my students.
- ❏ I will never forget: 'When in doubt—*don't!*'

2. Structure: *Building a Classroom— the foundation & fabric of learning!*

Principle—"A good teacher teaches students the subject, not the *subject* to students!"

Lesson I must learn: The more efficiently your classroom learning environment functions, the greater success you will have in promoting student achievement. Create a classroom where your students *want* to learn and *enjoy* coming to class. If you can do this, you will smooth the road to successful learning!

➤ Discipline by design!

➤ Expectations

➤ Anticipation: Closing the loopholes!

➤ Celebrating achievement: *Rewards*

➤ When all else fails…

"Peace is not the absence of conflict, but the ability to cope with conflict through peaceful means."

—President Ronald Reagan

Discipline by design!

Your students come first. As a teacher, in everything you do, remember— your students come *first*.

> Establish your discipline code early and take the first opportunity to enforce it. The atmosphere you establish in your classroom during the first two weeks will determine 90% of how your classroom functions the rest of the year.

Never forget that middle schoolers are children, however, and children very often see behavior management differently from you. The key word here is *management*. Middle schoolers tend to see the classroom as a democracy. It is actually a *benevolent dictatorship*. While students should be involved to some degree in the decision-making process, never let them forget that *you* are the one in charge.

Establish your discipline policy on day one. Until you establish a comfortable relationship with your students, you should begin strictly and ease up later. *The opposite approach is virtually impossible.*

Whatever type of discipline policy you choose to employ, make sure it is *clear, concise,* and *consistent.* If your students do not fully understand your expectations, you will create only confusion. If your expectations are complicated, your discipline policy will cause frustration and destroy the atmosphere of order you are trying to create. If you are inconsistent in enforcing your expectations, students will not take your policy seriously.

First, make sure your behavior management policy is *clear.* What is it you want? Make a list of desired behaviors and state clearly the behavior you expect your students to model. Be specific. Give the relevant information your students will need in order to meet your specific expectations. Never forget—if you expect it, *teach it.* You might even allow students to have some measure of input regarding the policies, but, whether or not you do this, you will find your policies to be more effective if they are clearly posted somewhere in your room. Clear expectations are also stated *specifically.* For example, say to your students, *"Bring to class your notebook and writing materials,"* instead of *"Come prepared for class."* Stating your behavior management policies in a positive, rather than negative, manner is also more effective. For example, say to your students, *"Let ME dismiss you when the bell rings, and you will have more travel time,"* instead of *"Don't jump up when the bell rings, or you will have to sit back down."* Remember that instructions are clear only if your students' *perspective* is clear!

During my first year of teaching, one of my lunch period students was experiencing behavior management difficulties in the cafeteria. When I could deal with it no more, I implored him to *"...behave in the lunchroom as you would behave in a restaurant!"* Sometime later, I saw the student with his parents at *McDonalds* and came to realize the way he had behaved in the cafeteria *was* the way he behaved in a restaurant! My expectation carried no challenge for the student since—through *his* perspective—it was permissible to *misbehave* in a public place. Always remember that your perspective—and the perspective of your students—may not always be the same!

Never be afraid to be honest and say, *"I don't know."* Middle schoolers appreciate sincerity.

Clarity of your discipline policy is also dependent on the *relevancy* of that policy. Be sure your students see the objectives or the relevancy in the desired behavior you seek to teach. In discussing desired behaviors with your students, ask them, *"Why is this important?"* Be sure they *understand* the importance—and the consequences of your policy. In this way, you can be sure they know the *reasoning* for your discipline policy. This better enables them to 'buy into' the policy, since they know its significance and relevance.

Clarity is also dependant on *understanding*—be sure students are clear on your classroom expectations. Say what you mean—mean what you say. Create a comfortable learning environment by inviting students to *"let me know if you don't understand."* Model and rehearse the behaviors whenever necessary and take note of your vocabulary. You must be sure your students heard what you thought you said and understood what you meant.

Second, make sure your discipline policy is *concise*. Brevity is not only the soul of wit—it's also the essence of good teaching! It is more effective to limit your behavior policy (or any lesson content!) to no more than 3 or 4 'digestible' pieces of information. Keep it simple, and above all, *teach* the behavior, *review* the behavior, and *practice* the behavior. Teaching, reviewing, and practicing behavior is as important as any other concept you will impress upon your students. Remember that instruction must not only be clear, it must be concise.

Third, make sure your discipline policy is *consistent*. Middle schoolers thrive on consistency, but consistency may not be something your students are used to. As with desired behaviors, you may also have to model consistency for them.

Remember the 20-30 minute attention spans.

In consistent discipline, teenagers see not only fairness, but also safety. Consistency in discipline means that you should never take misbehavior personally. Misbehavior isn't usually *about* you, even if it's directed *at* you. Be firm, but flexible, in your discipline. Set a strict standard and don't move the finish line. Also, remember that students act more often from impulse than evil.

If you are clear, concise and consistent in your behavior expectations, middle schoolers will generally respond positively to whatever discipline policy you employ.

We've discussed student behavior. Now, let's talk about *you*. What can you, as a teacher, do to aid in behavior management?

Let them think *your* plans are *their* idea...this works wonders!

Above all, become aware of your personal 'trigger points.' Trigger points are those points at which you will no longer tolerate an undesirable behavior. Be sure you recognize such trigger points *before* you become angry. Students will learn the limits of your tolerance as they measure your consistency and will generally stop short of behaviors that trigger consequences. Understand that students seldom desire to make you angry. Middle schoolers seek the comfort that established limits allow, and both you and your students must recognize the boundaries of those limits that you set in your classroom.

One spring, I took a group of elementary students outside for recreation/reward time and told them they could play anywhere on the playground. I did not clarify boundaries, and I noticed immediately that the children appeared insecure and hesitant to explore. Finally, I decided to establish boundaries for their play and placed large orange traffic cones as arbitrary boundaries that they were not to cross. *"Ok,"* I said, *"you may go anywhere within the orange cones—but you are not go past them."* Immediately, the children spread out within the boundaries and proceeded to enjoy their play. What they had needed was a well-defined limit and a clearly explained expectation. Given these, the children felt secure and became self-directed. Knowing the boundaries of your tolerance and establishing limits for student behavior will streamline whatever behavior management policy you employ.

> **LSD** works!: *love, structure*, and *discipline* are cardinal keys to middle school teaching!

Second, keep in mind that middle schoolers often react first and think later. Giving students an opportunity to cool off and correct themselves will usually solve more disciplinary problems than writing up every infraction. Give them their *space*—don't get in their face—when they overheat. Always demand respect, however. *Never* compromise on this expectation.

Third, decide beforehand how you will handle students without paper and pencils, tardies, excessive talking, gum, restroom breaks, lack of homework, etc., and *enforce* your policy. Make sure, however, that your consequences are appropriate, and not excessive. For example, do not write up every student who violates your gum rule, or forgets a pencil! This serves little purpose other than to make your point and overtax your office staff, and will create an adversarial atmosphere in your classroom. You must learn to *choose your battles*. Over-correction creates more problems than it solves.

> Middle schoolers get upset at *situations* more often than they get upset with you. Always try to give them an opportunity to back out of reactive rather than intentional misbehavior.

When you discuss your policies and procedures, explain the *why* and *reasoning* behind them. Think like a student in regard to rules—a rule without a reason is ridiculous. You will find students more cooperative if they understand the reasoning behind the rules. In whatever way you choose to handle your policies, be clear in expectation and consistent in enforcement. If possible, utilize reason over power. Never—*never* argue with students in front of a class, or make threats in anger. Keep private matters just *that!*

Sometimes, however, you have no choice but to enforce strict school discipline. Some infractions—such as violation of school rules—cannot be overlooked. Use, however, your authority sparingly and selectively. When you must discipline, make the discipline swift and effective. Also, make sure the punishment fits the infraction. Do not overcorrect, or under discipline. Never threaten, embarrass, berate, or humiliate a student. Always—*always* apologize when you're wrong. Praise *publicly* and admonish *privately*. Discipline the *behavior*; spare the child.

Finally, realize that there will be some students to whom you will not be their favorite teacher. Be realistic. You will not win the battle with every student, no matter hard you try. Nevertheless, clear and consistent discipline will, more than just about anything else, create a positive learning environment in a middle school classroom.

Expectations

Expectations. Set them high. Accept reality.

Years ago, the Western Electric Hawthorne Works in Cicero, Illinois discovered in the business world what teachers already knew. High expectations correlate with high achievement. The *Hawthorne Studies* (or *Hawthorne Experiments*) were conducted from 1927 to 1932, where Harvard Business School professor Elton Mayo examined productivity and work conditions. In essence, the *Hawthorne Effect* can be summarized by stating that student behaviors may be altered by the fact that students know there is a high expectation.

We all start the year with high expectations for our students, and rightly so. More often than not, your students will rise to meet the expectations you set, so set those expectations high. In a study known as *The Pygmalion Effect* by Rosenthal and Jacobson (1968), children aged six to twelve years, all drawn from the same school, were given an IQ test. Children were then assigned to an experimental or control group. When teachers were told that the children in the experimental group were "high achievers", expectations were increased. These children then began to show significant IQ gains over the course of one year, *despite* the allocation to a group having been, in fact, random. In other words, high expectations became self-fulfilling.

> Inspiration +
> Preparation +
> Motivation +
> Expectation =
> *Success!*

Remember the lessons of expectation. Research verifies that students gravitate toward the expectations set for them—whether those expectations are positive or negative! Learning *does* expand to fill expectations—expectations of the teacher—and expectations understood by students.

One year, I had a 5th period class with a large percentage of lower-functioning children. Somehow, the schedule had pooled them into that often 'drowsy' period that meets right after lunch. I decided I would modify—but not lower—my expectations for this class. I would tell the children I expected as much from them as from all my other classes. I raised the bar. At the end of the grading period, not only had this class met my expectations, they had exceeded them. They achieved *despite* limited abilities.

While expectation may not always lead to perfection, it will lead to positive achievement. But also accept reality. Know your students and the limits to their abilities. Do not set unachievable goals that will only frustrate them, but never fail to set genuinely high expectations for your students. Motivate your students to be *better* than they are.

Anticipation: Closing the loopholes!

The best cure is still prevention. This axiom is never proved truer than in your classroom. Close all loopholes for misbehavior *before* the misbehavior occurs, and your classroom will function far more efficiently. *Anticipate* the behavior patterns of your students, and you will make the teaching process much easier on yourself.

When you are ready to deviate from the traditional seating arrangement, wide short rows generally work best!

Seating charts, for example. Seating charts are most effectively used early in the year. They are a better *preventative* of misbehavior than *cure* for unacceptable conduct. You might do better to begin with the traditional *row* arrangement of desks until you learn student names and establish your authority in the classroom. Research has shown that the traditional arrangement *does* limit student interaction, and students placed in the *front* and *center* areas of the classroom will ask more questions. I like to seat my students across the *width*, rather than the *length* of the classroom. This creates the shortest distance between me and the back row of students. However you arrange your seating, be cognizant of *traffic patterns*. Middle schoolers gravitate to the path of *most* resistance when going from here to there. Close the loophole. Straighten the path. Eliminate the diversion and reduce your stress. If you establish seating charts early, your students will perceive them as an aid to taking roll, learning names, organizing cooperative learning activities, and enhancing behavior management. When used as a spontaneous punishment, however, your class may feel they are *all* being disciplined for the misbehavior of a few. *Anticipate.* Close this loophole.

> Never—never,
> leave students
> unsupervised in
> the classroom.

A second classroom management loophole to close is basic classroom logistics. Be sure your students know early where everything is—the pencil sharpener, Kleenex, assignment board, homework box, etc. Put your clock *behind* your students if possible. Let them know what is off-limits, such as your desk, the stapler, personal belongings, etc. Never assume they know. Teaching your students room logistics early prevents you from having to answer the same questions repeatedly later. (See Appendix: *How to survive opening day!*)

A third classroom management loophole I learned to close early was reducing the time consumed dealing with missed assignments for students who were absent. Instead of explaining numerous times about the prior day's assignment and what handouts were missed, I posted an 'assignment box' in the back of my room and attached it to the wall. When students return from an absence, they simply pick up the materials missed, which I place in the box. This requires my students to take personal responsibility for this aspect of their education. It also eliminates the opportunity for excuses and frees up my time by closing a loophole.

> It takes a middle schooler three times as long as it would take you to complete a task, and the effective *total* homework time for middle schoolers is ten minutes *times grade level*. Always make sure homework is authentic, meaningful, begun *in class* and *checked*. Also posting homework on free websites such as *Schoolnotes.com* is a fun and easy way to keep everyone at home abreast of the latest assignments, as well as interesting web pages!

A fourth classroom management loophole I learned to close was dealing with 'lost' materials left in my room. Instead of having children ask me a dozen times a day if I'd found a lost item, I created a '*Mr. Parks, did you find my...*' box where students always know I will put misplaced items.

A fifth classroom management loophole I closed was the collection of student assignments. Instead of having to collect and organize papers from my classes, I attached hourly class boxes to my walls. Students put their work in their class box. Time saved. Organization streamlined.

A sixth classroom management loophole I closed was to create a *'new student folder.'* New students generally arrive at your door with little or no notification. To have to restate all your beginning of the year expectations is as impractical as it is impossible. To maximize my time and the student's transition, I created a folder containing the syllabus for my class, expectations for my classroom, assessment procedures, etc. Again, time saved and organization streamlined.

A seventh classroom management loophole to close is what to do in emergency situations. Do you know how you will handle seizures, bee stings, and the administration of medications? Are you aware of *who* has epilepsy, allergic reactions, or asthma? Have you arranged for your sub to know this information? Remember confidentialities. Know the policies regarding what you can and cannot do in emergencies, and be prepared. Emergencies *will* happen.

Reward for good behavior. Do not bribe students to 'be good' for a reward.

An eighth classroom management loophole to close is to realize that your students will sometimes have problems you simply cannot—and should not—deal with. In cases of suspected abuse, severe depression, or suicidal tendencies, etc., refer students to the counselor. Never forget that you are a teacher—not a psychologist. Don't attempt to solve every problem your students bring to you. Let the professionals deal with the serious ones.

A ninth classroom loophole to close is to eliminate the temptation to meddle! Middle schoolers are extremely curious, and chalk next to the chalkboard, or colorful markers next to the whiteboard are sometimes impossibly tempting! Keep these out of sight. Too, keep in mind that if students are writing on your desks, it is generally due to boredom. Consider this.

A final classroom loophole to close is what I call *'management through proximity.'* This often forgotten and highly effective tool recognizes the importance of you, as the teacher, moving throughout your classroom. Students will behave in a more positive manner when you do not remain stationary. Along these lines, always maintain a 'scan-desk' mentality as you teach. That is, never become so lesson-focused that you don't continually scan the room for problems that may be waiting to happen. Keep your eyes *open* to *close* this loophole. A working 'scan-desk' mentality 'defrags' a multitude of potential difficulties! Management through proximity. Simple, but effective.

Anticipate—close the loopholes. Always keep in mind regarding behavior management when dealing with middle schoolers—an ounce of prevention is *better* than a pound of cure! Anything you can do to avoid difficulties will streamline the process and make your classroom a more pleasant and enjoyable environment for all.

Celebrating achievement: Rewards

While every teacher would like to believe that students learn for the joy of learning, realistically this applies to the very few. Let's face it—the majority of your students would rather be somewhere else besides sitting in your classroom. In dealing with middle schoolers, even the most dynamic teaching personality has its limit and teachers must find other ways to keep students motivated.

> Talking *with* is memorable. Talking *to* is instructive. Talking *at* is sedating! *If you awaken their interest, and stir their curiosity, you will multiply their learning!* Enthusiasm is highly contagious—so also, is apathy and boredom. *Remember, kids sometimes will find more learning in your light, than in your lesson.*

While attending an NMSA conference one year, I recall hearing a speaker say, *"Teaching is a selling profession. We are selling a product called education, and the more enticing we make this product to our buyers, the greater will be our successes!"* Whatever may be your personal philosophy on the subject—rewards *do* motivate—especially in middle school! Celebrating achievement builds interest in the classroom, and *interested* students learn more efficiently.

Rewards must be age-appropriate. What is positive reinforcement to older teens may not work for younger students. But remember that middle schoolers are still children. Very often, the most effective way to enter a student's mind is through a child's heart—and sometimes, through a child's *stomach!*

> Remember when keeping treats—some students may be diabetic, allergic to certain foods, or have braces. Keep some snacks 'just in case.'

I have found that a few small candy bars used as a reward in review-question activities makes this activity not only more effective, but also more enjoyable. Several times a month, I play the *Jeopardy* review game with my middle schoolers. Students try to formulate a correct question for any answer I give them. A candy bar is the reward.

I am always amazed at how hard my students will work for chocolate! Not only does this make learning enjoyable, it is also *performance based.* Performance based learning stimulates higher-level thinking skills. Instead of merely choosing a response (as in the typical review game format) students are forced to generate an inquiry.

While you may feel that rewarding students might tend to reduce intrinsic motivation, research has shown this not to be the case. Never forget—you are dealing with children, and recognition or reward is a wonderful reinforcement tool. Stickers, treats, awards, etc., really *will* motivate middle schoolers, and are tools you can and should use in your classroom.

Whatever rewards you choose to employ, remember—do not *overuse* them. Rewards should be anticipated, but not assumed. Make sure your students see rewards as reinforcement for positive behavior, not bribes to avoid negative consequences. Overuse of rewards produces ever-diminishing returns. Used sparingly, rewards can bait the hook of learning and motivate your students to achieve. Celebrate achievement! It motivates your students!

When all else fails...

Although you control most aspects of management in your classroom, there will be times when such control slips out of your hands. Changes in the schedule, lessons that flop, unexpected weather and fire drills, fights in the hall, your unanticipated need for a sub, spontaneous assemblies—all of these will occur when you least expect them. When they do, the best behavior management technique is to abandon your prepared plan and change course. Therefore, always—*always* have a 'plan B'.

Use mnemonic devices. Middle schoolers love these!

A 'plan B' will keep things at least on a functioning plane until things return to an even keel. As a new teacher, the last thing you need is to have to devise an alternative lesson in the midst of a crisis or unexpected change in routine. Be proactive—have an emergency or 'anytime' lesson prepared, and make sure whoever is going to need it (including you!) will know where to locate it!

The least I need to know: My to do checklist!

- ❑ I will remember that my students are children first.
- ❑ I will remember that my students will enjoy my class more if they see I truly enjoy what I do!

- ❏ I will set *clear, concise,* and *consistent* expectations for my students, and state them in a positive manner.
- ❏ I will remember that my students may often not hear exactly what I meant to say!
- ❏ I will strive to create a safe and inviting atmosphere in my classroom where my students are not afraid to ask questions when they do not understand.
- ❏ I will practice flexibility and fairness in my behavior management and give my students the opportunity to correct their own behavior.
- ❏ I will never discipline in haste or anger, and will correct *behaviors* rather than *persons.*
- ❏ I will never argue with, threaten, or humiliate my students.
- ❏ I will require my students to respect my *position* as teacher, even if I'm not their *favorite* teacher.
- ❏ I will never compare my students, or play favorites!
- ❏ I will practice *listening* to the opinions and reasoning of my students.
- ❏ I will recognize my own 'trigger points', learn to pick my battles, and to overlook the small stuff.
- ❏ I will learn how to apologize to students when I'm wrong and compliment them when they're right.
- ❏ I will be proactive in closing classroom loopholes before they lead to unacceptable consequences.
- ❏ I will understand my students' view of rewards and practice rewards in a timely manner.
- ❏ I will always have a *'Plan B'* just in case!

3. Support: *Building Parental Resources—help is out there!*

Principle—"Your most valuable resource is the one you will most seldom use!"

Lesson I must learn: The parents of your students are an invaluable resource. Utilize and appreciate them at every opportunity, and you will gain the most important ally you will ever have as a teacher!

> ➤ A short course in dealing with parents.

A short course in dealing with parents

Without question, the most important resources you will have are resources that you seldom see in your classroom. Those resources are the parents of your students. Parents are your students' *first* teachers.

As a newer teacher, you may prefer less contact with parents. Many teachers see parents and parent questions as a challenge to their authority. This, however, is destructive to the parent/teacher relationship. Parents are not opponents, but allies. When parents have questions, let them know such questions are welcomed. Never forget—their concern is for *their* child. Your concern is for them *all*. Recognize that whatever you can do to help parents make *your* job easier will prove to be time well spent.

The school environment often intimidates parents, but they are the allies you *cannot* afford to be without. Make it a point to invite them to your school. Include them in class activities that involve their children. Provide them with a syllabus of your class and a calendar of school events. Encourage them. They are your most valuable resource. (See Appendix: *When conferencing with parents.*)

Always remember to return parents' phone calls and emails, and do so promptly.

I have found it to be helpful in recruiting the assistance of parents to begin every year with a handout of parent helps entitled *Chicken Soup for Parenting*, which I have included in the appendix of this book. This mini-instruction manual which deals with homework, Internet resources, study time, etc., gives parents a head start on helping *me* become a more effective teacher of their children.

A second thing I do to involve parents is always to make it a policy to contact them before they need to contact me. Because of the middle school design, teachers tend to have more frequent contact with homeroom parents than parents of students in other classes. Nevertheless, I try to send some type of positive correspondence (in addition to progress reports) to parents of every student I teach. This is time-consuming, and sometimes impractical, but the bottom line is—it simply builds good rapport.

For example, to the parents of students who excel academically in my class, or students who seldom receive discipline reports or failing grades, I send home a 'your child is a pleasure to teach letter.' (See Appendix: *Sample positive parent contact*) Time and time again, I have been told by parents that they never receive *positive* correspondences from teachers, and that these letters have been copied and sent to grandma, or taped on refrigerators and kitchen bulletin boards. To parents, this simple, positive contact is unexpected evidence that someone appreciates his or her child. Surprise your students' parents—tell them something *good*. You will gain an ally you cannot afford to be without.

A third thing I do to involve parents in a positive way is to mail home an official school discipline report on a student who exhibits wonderful behavior in my classroom. Instead of describing an offense, however, I will fill in notes of appreciation and praise. The parent is caught by surprise when the 'official' school letter arrives. This action—used sparingly—has proved a positive icebreaker to more parents than I can number.

A fourth thing I do to involve parents is to utilize their careers. Although there will be exceptions, parents generally enjoy coming into my classroom and speaking about what they do for a profession. Don't forget to tell them ahead of time how much time will be available to them, and remember to videotape presentations. Parents may be able to present to only one class. This will enable you to reuse the presentation in other classes, and in future years. *Always* send them a thank you note. Even if parents decline such invitations, you have established an 'open-door' policy, and when parents feels free to communicate with you, you gain tremendous leverage.

> Teaching carries with it an unstated expectation that the student has a problem, and the teacher has the solution.

A fifth way to involve parents is to begin each year collecting email addresses. More and more parents are becoming available through email. You will find that being able to contact a parent by email regarding a student's grade or conduct is quite helpful. Parents are far more likely to keep in contact with you through email than by telephone. Email correspondence is also more documentable, and documenting everything is an understood rule in middle school. (See Appendix: *Important documents to keep!*)

A sixth way to involve parents is to invite them to assist you as an aide in your classroom. Allow them to judge exhibitions or projects. Many parents are also quite willing to help with class and school announcements, copying hand-outs, sorting files, tutoring and monitoring students, etc.

Finally, consider a school (or team) newsletter. Sending home a monthly newsletter with student-parent challenges, digital photos of students, and timely articles of what is going on at school is a personal and much-appreciated contact.

Empower your students' parents! In allowing them to help you help their children, you recognize them as a valuable ally and build a unique team relationship.

The least I need to know: My to do checklist!

- ❑ I will remember that parents are my most valuable allies, allies I *cannot* afford to be without.
- ❑ I will try to utilize the skills of parents rather than perceive them as the opposition.
- ❑ I will make it a policy to, in some way, contact parents regarding something positive before parents end up needing to contact me.
- ❑ I will send home *thank you notes* whenever they are necessary.
- ❑ I will create at least the atmosphere of an open-door policy toward parents.
- ❑ I will attempt to make my classroom an inviting—not intimidating—place where parents will feel comfortable in coming.
- ❑ I will collect as many email contacts from parents as I am able.

4. Maintenance: *Building Relationships— functioning successfully in the school environment!*

Principle—"Everything you needed to know to become a teacher—they *didn't* teach you at the university!"

Lesson I must learn: 'Big doors often swing on small hinges.' There are small but important things you must remember in order to become a successful teacher, and the way you deal with your staff, duties, and personal responsibilities will determine your success or failure as a teacher. Learn these lessons well!

> ➢ Your two biggest assets within the building!
> ➢ *"And never the twain shall meet!"*
> ➢ The Proactive solution
> ➢ Think before you speak!
> ➢ You'd better take them seriously: *Responsibilities*
> ➢ Substitutes

Your two biggest assets within the building!

As a new teacher, you must understand the school environment and personnel that will comprise your home away from home for as long as you teach. The first thing to understand is the distinction between *certified* and *classified* staff. While certified staff (teachers and administrators) may be considered the so-called brains of the school, the classified staff is truly the heart and soul. Get to know your classified staff well. *Appreciate* them even more.

Your most valuable assets among classified staff are—without a doubt—the secretary in the front office and the custodian. Little can be achieved during the course of a school day without them. Make it a practice to do small things to improve their day. Remember to say 'thank you,' and treat them with respect when you enter their domain. Understand that this is their turf, and they don't work for you.

Atmosphere is your first and most important creation. Middle schoolers *thrive* on challenge, but *freeze* on threat. Remember, if the tone is pleasant, you can be off-key a few times, and the song will still be remembered!

For example, don't wait to do something nice for the secretary (or secretaries) on 'Secretary's Day.' The school will probably do that. Let them know you appreciate them more than once a year. Send them a note of appreciation for no special occasion. Leave them a sweet treat to surprise them, and be sure to bring them a small gift when you attend conferences. Remember how busy they are, and try not to inundate them with requests for things you may be able to do for yourself. Remember to answer the phone in a pleasant manner when you are interrupted in the middle of your perfect lesson—it may be a busy secretary (or a parent!) simply needing information. Return, in a timely manner, such things as your morning attendance list, surveys, locker combinations, purchase orders, and receipts. Failing to do these makes their jobs more difficult. What you may perceive to be mundane or insignificant becomes exponentially more difficult for them when multiplied by the number of teachers involved. Remember, these people keep the school functioning, and they have deadlines too. The effectiveness of their job is not separate from, but often *dependent* on you doing your part in the process. Learn to appreciate your secretaries. They are your most valuable personnel assets.

Your second most valuable personnel asset is the custodian. Without the custodians, *you* would be fixing what was broken and cleaning up the accidents in the hall. Without the custodians your room this morning would look the way you left it yesterday afternoon. Practice small acts of courtesy toward your custodians. For example, I always try to straighten my students' desks and pick up much of the stuff kids leave on my floor *before* the custodian comes in. If your room has tables with chairs, be sure the students put the chairs up before they leave if your custodian prefers this. This will make his or her job easier, and you will feel less intrusive the next time you misplace your keys and need your room opened!

Never forget—you have one room to deal with for nine months—your custodians have dozens to deal with year round. They are the experts in building management and take pride in its appearance. Always ask their help when making permanent changes in facets of the building, such as drilling holes for pencil sharpeners, putting nails in walls, etc.

"And never the twain shall meet!"

Your school environment, of course, includes more than merely the secretaries and the custodians. Your school environment is your home away from home. The key here is the word 'away'. A second way you relate to your school environment is how it is affected by what goes on at home. In your school environment, it is vitally important that you remember to never mix concerns at home with responsibilities at school. This is not always easy.

Sometimes that lesson in your 6th period class falls flat, and you think about your poor planning for it all the way home. Sometimes that disagreement with your spouse or children at home follows you to school, and your day starts off on a down note. Sometimes mixing home and school concerns is simply unavoidable, but, whenever possible, try to keep home and school problems separated.

Bringing home problems to school can affect your teaching. Middle schoolers are especially perceptive and often pick up on things we may not expect.

> **Accept the fact that your energy level *decreases*, and your weight generally *increases* during your first year. Eat with this in mind!**

Try to smile often. Smiling does affect your tone of voice and middle schoolers are especially responsive to voice tone. It is not possible to always be a bundle of joy when you come into your classroom, but you can at least be cheerful toward your students. Your classroom demeanor and effectiveness as a teacher can be easily affected when things at home affect things at school. Too, you may more readily say something you do not mean, or perhaps lose patience more quickly, when you are tired because problems at home are affecting your job at school. Keep these two domains separated as much as you are able.

In the same way, try not to take your school problems home. You will have difficulty enough with the schoolwork you *must* take home—try not to add problems at school to the load! Your family deserves your full attention as well. Treating school concerns and home concerns as separate emotional environments will go a long way to lengthening your career as a teacher!

The Proactive solution

Another way you relate to your school environment is your attitude towards it and all that environment entails. You will do well to develop a *proactive* attitude. Becoming a proactive teacher in your attitude, actions, and appearance will reap greater rewards for you than just about anything else you can do. You can become a proactive teacher in a number of simple—but highly effective—ways.

For example, take the initiative to arrive early to school. It just looks good. Many teachers habitually arrive at school five minutes before homeroom begins. While there may be nothing inherently wrong with this, you will make a positive and lasting impression on your administration and fellow teachers if you make it a point to arrive early. Arriving early also makes you available in case you are needed. Not only can you get more lesson preparation done early in the morning than you would on a busy afternoon, but you'll probably never raise an eyebrow on those days when it becomes necessary for you to leave school early.

A second proactive habit is to invite your administrators (and parents) into your classroom before they come out of necessity. If you create an open-door policy to your classroom, you will feel less intimidated by unannounced visits and visits for purposes of evaluation.

A third proactive habit is to always pay back other teachers with interest. What does this mean? Whenever you borrow items from other teachers, such as paper, paper clips, folders, etc., always return *more* than you borrowed. Pay back 'with interest.' Whenever a teacher covers an obligation or duty for you, don't simply repay the favor—repay it as soon as possible! Payback with interest is a small action that will be remembered.

> One of the most effective learning devices you can use to stimulate higher level thinking skill is the analogy. For example, have students complete such analogical thinking paradigms as, 'sixty is to six, as a dollar is to what?' Another might be, 'thermometer is to temperature, as (what) is to weight?' Or, 'Homer is to (what) as Shakespeare is to *Julius Caesar?*' The use of *metaphor, allegory,* and *comparison/contrast* prompts also show high correlation with student achievement.

A fourth proactive habit is to never leave school without at least a start on what tomorrow requires. I am a morning person and plan my day's activities better in the morning than on the afternoon of the day before. But I always strive at least to *begin* the next day's activities before I leave school. This enables me to fine-tune the lesson in my mind before I teach it the next day. Remember, everything you don't put off today becomes unnecessary to do tomorrow!

A fifth proactive habit is to take the initiative to introduce yourself to all personnel in the building without waiting for them to come to you. Know where these people are in your building. The librarians, counselors, coaches, cafeteria workers, the school nurse (if you have one)—all are intricate parts of your professional environment. Get to know them. You will need favors from all of them eventually.

A sixth proactive habit is to volunteer for committees and school duty, rather than waiting to be asked. Such are time-consuming, but they are an intricate part of the teaching duty. They are things you have to do, so look more professional—volunteer! Don't sit and wait to be assigned.

Finally, become proactive in your monitoring of student behavior and activity outside your immediate classroom. Be in the halls between classes. Check restrooms and other areas in your school where students might linger. Don't wait to be asked (or told!). Be proactive. *Just do it!*

A proactive attitude looks good, accomplishes much, and reaps innumerable benefits. Find as many ways as you can to become *proactive* rather than *reactive*! If you will strive to 'do without having to be asked,' you will reap dividends many times over for the small effort it requires.

Think before you speak

Yet another way you relate to your school environment is through the words that come out of your mouth. Someone has said that our words will get us into trouble long before our actions cause us grief. This is never truer than in a middle school environment. Be very careful what you say around—and about—staff and students. Your words may come back to haunt you.

A middle school is its own microcommunity. It is made up of individuals from different backgrounds, different beliefs, and different personalities. What may be funny to one person may be hurtful or even offensive to

> The element of *surprise* is one of the most important things you can utilize in a middle school classroom! Keeping them on their toes is fascinating, exciting, and effective! *Routine* is the substance of a middle-schooler's life. They thrive on *consistency*, and consistency makes the occasional *diversion* that much more exciting!

another. A confidence meant to be kept may damage a reputation if that confidence is betrayed. A rumor spread can create a lasting animosity, and idle conversations may make you enemies.

Always be mindful of *where* you are. Be careful what you say inside—as well as outside—your classroom. As teachers, we become so accustomed to being surrounded we sometimes neglect to see students—or worse, parents—who might overhear a conversation and repeat what we prefer to be kept private. Remember, too, that middle schoolers are children who not only repeat what is heard, but often misunderstand and misquote what they hear.

As a teacher, you are also dealing with an adult staff with which you will be spending many years. Think *carefully* before you speak. Is this conversation inappropriate? Is this conversation unnecessary? Is it something that could be no more than idle gossip? Is this an adult concern that should not be shared with students? Is this something that could be misinterpreted or misconstrued? Reputations—including yours—can be easily damaged by such indiscretions of conversation. If you do have a 'disagreement' with a colleague—air out your differences. Respectfully resolve them as soon as possible. *Never* let them fester! Never pre-judge what you may not fully understand. Listen twice as often as you speak. If there is *any* doubt regarding whether or not you should say something, you will do well to leave it unsaid! It is always easier to defend what you *didn't* say.

Finally, be aware of the attitude you might be conveying to those you work with. Remember, *you* are the new teacher with much to learn. You will be much better accepted by conveying a humble and compliant attitude than by coming off as defensive and pedantic. While you may be fresh out of school, you don't have to act like it!

You'd better take them seriously...

A final way you relate to your school environment is in your performance of duties. As a new teacher, you will learn that teaching is like an iceberg. Dealing with students is merely the tip of a much larger responsibility—the most time-consuming of which involves meetings and conferences. While these may not be as exciting as what you do in the classroom, they are just as much a part of your job description, and you'd better take them seriously.

For example, if you are a part of a middle school team, you may meet with other team members on a regular basis. At times, you might feel as though you could be using your time more efficiently by doing lesson preparation. Nevertheless, you would do well not to opt out of such meetings unless absolutely necessary. The same holds true for department meetings, detention, bus supervision, Admission and Release Committee (ARC) meetings, school committee meetings, and especially parent-teacher conferences. Some of these duties will require after-school time, but take them seriously and attend. Your peers probably feel the same way you do about them, but for the most part, they will be there, and you should be, too. It looks good, and it's an understood part of your job description.

Faithfulness in the performance of school duties not only *looks* more professional—it *is* more professional.

Substitutes

When you cannot be in your classroom, it is more than simple courtesy to leave your substitute detailed and clear lesson plans. It is also the *professional* thing to do. Don't forget to tell them bell schedules, attendance and discipline policies, and whom to seek on your team if they need help. I also try leave instructions about weather emergencies and how these are dealt with by school policy. My classroom policies—hall passes, restroom and locker breaks, etc. are all listed for the sub. However, I generally request they do not collect homework. This eliminates all possibility of my students claiming that the homework they didn't do was lost by the sub! I keep a folder in which I include those documents as well as seating charts, lists of students they can trust, any medical issues that might arise, and lunch procedures. Make sure your students know that when a substitute is teaching in your absence, you are expecting them to be on their best behavior. Let them know their conduct reflects upon you as their teacher.

Substitutes have a difficult job. Do what you can to make their job easier. I also try to also leave a snack or two for subs in my classroom refrigerator.

The least I need to know: My to do checklist!

- ❑ I will make it a practice to show small kindnesses to the secretaries and custodians, and to always treat them with respect.
- ❑ I will make a conscious effort not to mix problems at home with work at school.
- ❑ I will strive to be among the first teachers to arrive at school in the morning and among the last teachers to leave in the afternoon!
- ❑ I will make it a habit to pay back with interest those who lend me things.
- ❑ I will try to get at least a start on tomorrow's lesson before I leave school today!

❑ I will be very careful what I say at school, and I will not spread gossip or rumors.

❑ I will remember to leave my substitute full and courteous preparation.

5. Content: *Building a Lesson—the bricks and mortar of learning!*

Principle—"An ounce of need will go further than a pound of content!"

Lesson I must learn: Your familiarity with the subject you teach—and the way you present the information—is the heart and soul of your job. Know your content, and distribute it in a way that is easily digestible to the children you teach!

- ➤ '*Nice* to know or *need* to know?'
- ➤ The Big Picture!
- ➤ The *Bloom*-ing miracle!
- ➤ The 3 '*R*'s!
- ➤ The Socrates Effect!
- ➤ Assessment

Nice to know or need to know?

To fail to plan is to plan to fail. It's as simple as this—effective teachers prepare effective lessons.

In preparing effective lessons, your first consideration regarding the information you teach your students is *relevancy*. Are you preparing to teach what you are *supposed* to be teaching? Is this lesson information a part of your subject core content? Is this lesson applicable to the state and national standards in your subject area, or 'filler material,' e.g., stuff *you* enjoy? Understand that *education*—not entertainment—is the job with which you are entrusted and that students do recognize the distinction. While non-curricular information can be interesting as an occasional diversion, never forget—you are being paid, and trusted—to teach the curriculum. *Need to know* always takes precedence over *nice to know*, and you must never allow important information to become victim to the trivial.

Teaching your curriculum presupposes that you *know* your curriculum. It is critical that you become proficient in the curriculum area of the subject you teach. If you know your curriculum, you will be better able to make lesson connections, which are vital to the ability of your students to generalize and apply information. Stay abreast of current research and updates in your area. Volunteer for curriculum committees, test writing, textbook reviews, etc. (See Chapter 1: *Professionalism.*) This will enable you to know and apply your core content, and understand what is expected of you in your classroom. Be *very* familiar with your state's required teaching for core content in your subject. You should also know the content and concepts for the grade levels before and following yours so that you can connect and lay the foundations for those concepts as well.

Look up and become familiar with the National Standards. You are expected to do no less as a professional, even if you are not directly held accountable to do so. The increasing emphasis on state testing of students may expose your weaknesses if you do not teach what your students need to know. *You must establish credibility with your students!* Students need to know the core content of the subject content you teach, and—just as importantly—they need to know *you* know it.

The Big Picture!

Preparing lessons is not an art. It is an acquired skill. It takes practice, but is not difficult. (See Appendix: *Sample Lesson Plan*) One way to make prepared lessons more effective is to utilize the 'scope and sequence' method in your lesson design. Ask yourself *"what is the overall goal of this lesson?"* In other words, what are the *essential questions* you want your students to be able to answer? Once you have established that within acceptable parameters for the age group you teach, proceed to break down the process by which you will achieve this. Make sure you see the *sum* before you develop the *parts.*

The scope and sequence method also aids your students as well. Tell your students what it is you will be teaching them. Keep them aware of where they've been and where you're taking them. When students know and understand the scope and sequence of a lesson, they are better able to stay focused, set goals, and ask essential questions.

I have found it helpful to both students and parents to provide a syllabus reflecting the units, concepts, and topics to be covered in my class during the year, along with when each unit will be taught. Whether or not your school requires a yearly syllabus, it is still an excellent personal organizer to help you, your students, and their parents understand what you will be teaching.

The Bloom-ing miracle!

While we're on the subject of your lesson, consider the simplest—and yet most effective—method you will ever encounter in its creation and delivery. This method was conceived by Aristotle, is universal in its acceptance, and, in truth, comprises the heart and soul of eighty per cent of all the educational research on effective teaching and learning. It's called *Bloom's Taxonomy of Learning*, and it's the finest frame on which you will ever construct a lesson. The taxonomy is hierarchical, that is, it begins in simplicity and advances through complexity. Its foundation goes back to the ancient Greek method of instruction—a method that still works today. I have included a basic structure of the use of Bloom's Taxonomy in the *Appendix* of this book. Study the hierarchy. Utilize the structure. Plan and construct around its framework and your students will benefit greatly. This taxonomy is probably the finest single paradigm of teaching and learning ever created.

The 3 'R's!

A final element in effective lesson preparation is to understand the audience to whom you will be teaching the lesson.

Application is everything! If the lesson isn't *applied* to their world, it's as relevant as a rock. The only application more important to them than present-day application is *personal* application! Never let a 'teachable moment' pass without milking it for all it's worth! *APPLY, APPLY, and APPLY!* "An ounce of need is better than a pound of content!"

Middle schoolers have unique mindsets. Their retention spans and interest levels are far different from yours. They generally tend to live in the 'immediate' and have difficulty generalizing concepts and applying lessons as we would like them to. Because such adolescent characteristics often work against that perfectly planned lesson you created, you would do well to remember the 3 'R's' of teaching a lesson to middle schoolers.

First, your lesson must *relate*. While relating your lesson to prior knowledge, or to another subject in your curriculum is important, your lessons will prove *most* effective when they relate to some thread of relevancy in your students' lives. Middle schoolers relate through *internalizing* information, and internalization is tied to *importance*. As much as *you* might value your lesson, that lesson will generally rate no higher than *sixth* on your students' priority list! The most important priorities in a teenager's life rank something like this: *themselves*, their *friends*, their *family*, their *peers*, and *you*— or the teacher at the moment. The lesson you prepared so carefully is low on their priority list and may rank somewhere down there with *"what time is it?"* or *"when does the bell ring?"* Relate your lesson to that which is important in your students' lives.

Remember, if the lesson doesn't relate to something *else* on their priority list, it won't be effective.

One teacher tells the story of how she was waxing eloquent in her most brilliant lesson—captivating (she thought) her audience—holding their attention in the palm of her hand. Suddenly, a student with a surprised look flashing across his face raised his hand to ask the penetrating question, *"Have we had lunch yet?"* Such is the attention span of a middle schooler.

Middle schoolers can only absorb fifteen minutes or so of information, and their attention spans are about twice their chronological age, so if you want information remembered, you'd better make that information *relevant!* Something in your lesson must *matter* to them. The best way to relate your lesson is to recognize a channel for their interests and work to fill it!

> "Teach a lesson, mold a character, shape a destiny."

In social studies, for example, the concepts of *change over time* and *historical perspective* are fundamental concepts students must learn. Understanding that the likes, dislikes, and opinions of teenagers also change much over time, I wanted to find a channel through which I could relate the concept. I decided to let them make a *time capsule*. Early in the year, each student filled out a prepared form where they could list popular songs, movies, and events from the beginning of school. I also permitted them to include private things such as whom they liked (certain to change over time!), predictions of grades, and best friends. In a big 'burial' ceremony, the form was then sealed in an envelope and taped into a 'secret' part of their notebook. (I also discovered fewer notebooks were lost during the year!) At some later time, I had the students open their time capsule, and as the students laughed at how *"different things are now!"* the 'change over time' lesson became quite relevant! Why? It related to things important to them. I had recognized a channel for their interests and worked to fill it! The lesson *related*.

The next best way to relate your lesson is to connect it to a current event. For example, during our study of Mesopotamia, we experienced the tragedy of September 11, 2001. Rather than forcing my prepared lesson on confused children, I chose to link the day's events to the history of that troubled area of the world. In doing this, the lesson became far more memorable. *Relate* the lesson and you will impress the learning.

Following these two, the next best way to relate the lesson is to connect it to prior knowledge. Prior knowledge helps the mind categorize information, therefore making it more retainable. Prior knowledge might be nothing more than yesterday's lesson, but it helps middle schoolers see the aim, purpose, and flow of the lesson, rather than appearing to them as mere learning for the sake of learning. However you do it, remember—effective lessons *relate*.

> **Research indicates that learning retention rate increases from 35-52% as material is practiced through 3-5 repetitions. We remember 10% of what we hear. We remember 50% of what we hear and see. We remember 90% of what we hear, see, *and* do.**

Second, you should never be afraid to *repeat* your lesson. Repeating a lesson does not mean you teach the same lesson over and over. It means that you repeat and rephrase *key concepts* of each lesson in order to make the impression. Your students may complain, but through continual repetition you will hear your lesson in their voices and quickly learn if what they understood was what you *thought* they understood!

A teacher tells of teaching 6th graders the concept of ancestor worship in the Orient. In reviewing for the test, she made it a point to remind students to review that concept. When students were later asked to discuss the subject in a narrative, many expressed the esteem with which the people in the Orient held their sisters and other female members of their families. The teacher was puzzled by these numerous comments until she realized the children had no concept of the term 'ancestors'! They thought she had been referring to their 'aunts' and 'sisters'!

> **Never assume they know! If you're lucky, they'll ask questions! It's better to explain the details again and again, than to build on a foundation that isn't there.**

In teaching social studies to middle schoolers, I assumed that my students understood the words to the *Pledge of Allegiance*—something they had repeated each morning for half their lives. I was wrong. While all knew the words, most did not understand the terms 'allegiance' or 'indivisible'. Half their lives. They never knew.

Never assume that all your students understood what you *thought* they understood. While most may, many will not. If you're *lucky*, they ask questions. Most won't. Remember that *repetition is never redundant*—it's the mother of learning! Very often, it helps you clarify misunderstanding you might never have anticipated.

Another teacher, teaching in a farming community, tells of spending an entire class period teaching 6th graders various phases of agricultural development in another culture. Assuming the lesson to be going well, the teacher asked if there were any questions. Following an excruciatingly long wait, one student raised his hand and asked, *"What is agriculture?"* Redirecting the question, the teacher asked if someone else could explain the term. No one could. Finally surrendering, the teacher gave the class a simple definition of the term. Suddenly, the lights of learning flashed across the faces in her class, and one student replied: *"Well, now it makes sense!"*

> **"It is more effective to question the answers than to answer the questions!"**

Third, make it a habit to continually *review* your lesson. Middle schoolers love to show what they know—especially when an occasional reward is on the line. I have had success with *Jeopardy* answer and question oral reviews, and always keep a supply of miniature candy bars in my desk to raise the stakes once in a while.

One of my favorite review activities is a reciprocal teaching technique I call *'the power of the chalk.'* I challenge willing students to 'teach the board,' upon which I have left the previous day's lesson. I sit in the student's seat, and the student takes my place reviewing the board—chalk in hand. In giving my students the power of the chalk, I learn how effective—or *ineffective*—was the prior lesson. As I sit as a student, I am able to refocus and clarify when necessary. Students love this activity and the 'authority' it gives them! Be prepared, however—this activity will expose every part of your lesson that was misunderstood or *unclear* to your students. More than once I have been amazed that what students understood was *not* what I intended to convey! You can never review too often in middle school!

Relate the lesson to check for understanding, *Repeat* the lesson to transform short-term memory into long-term memory, and *Review* the lesson for internalization! These are vital parts of effective lesson planning and teaching.

The Socrates Effect!

Your lesson is only as good as the impact it makes on student learning. Do not see your lesson as mere information to be converted into a teaching 'bullet' and fired at your students! This is *not* teaching. Teaching involves more than delivery of information. Teaching involves creating a new perspective in the thoughts and minds of your students.

Socrates was a famous Greek philosopher. He was also an effective teacher. Socrates taught—not through delivery of information—but through stimulation of *inquisitiveness.* Instead of filling a vacuum with information, he *created* a vacuum of challenge into which the natural inquisitiveness of his students plunged! In a teaching technique that bears his name today, Socrates forced his students to come to their own conclusions by means of skilled questioning methods—the *Socratic method.*

Learn how to question your students in ways that will enable them to *reason, analyze,* and *apply infor-mation.* Challenge their minds by making them *explain,* not just answer. For example, in my social studies class, I try to ask more *why* than *what* questions. I ask students to paraphrase or rephrase—not just repeat—information and concepts learned in class. When a student asks a question, try asking another student to *rephrase* that question. In doing so, you not only generate thinking, you also check for understanding. Later, as your students come to conclusions, inquire as to possible *effects* and *alternatives* of their conclusions. Ask them to *defend* statements they make in class by citing *examples.* Instead of merely feeding information to your students, try challenging them with questions that force them to *analyze* and *explain.* You will be pleased with the increased retention rate!

> Always practice *wait time* after you question. Research shows that learning is stimulated through the extended pause following a question. As the *wait time* increases, so does student learning!

> Grades do not *fully* reflect either teaching or learning well. Grades are only as good as the assessment system that formulates them, and should *never* be a tool of behavior modification. Sometimes, keeping the score is not as important as cheering the process!

Assessment

Student assessment is a necessary and important part of teaching. It can, however, sometimes be intimidating for students and can create a 'you against us' attitude between students and teacher. This attitude, you need to change as early in the year as possible. Be sure you go over your assessment procedures

> **Studies have shown that retention rate *decreases* as assessment paradigms are utilized in the following order: *personalized, analytical thinking, hands-on, conceptual material, factual material, irrelevant material.* Authentic assessment that relates is the finest assessment of all. Assessing does not need to be depressing in the middle school classroom and however you create relaxation during assessment, remember— students who are relaxed assess more efficiently.**

with your students early in the year, and review them often. Be sure you post your grading scale for students to see. It is important to make sure assessments are not perceived as something negative. Testing is to make sure students understood the objectives of an assignment. If your students learn to not perceive assessment as something negative and intimidating, you will create a more relaxed assessment atmosphere, and students who are relaxed assess more efficiently.

Early in my teaching career, I noticed that test-taking was almost always perceived by students as a negative experience. I wanted to change this perception, but how could I make the dreaded test-taking process enjoyable?

First, I had to consider my audience. I was dealing with middle school children, where, more often than not, the more off-the-wall the activity, the more enjoyable they find it!

Second, I needed to choose an aspect of test taking to employ my activity. I knew middle schoolers often hurt themselves on quizzes by misnumbering answers, or failing to include their name. In an effort to eliminate these occurrences, I created my 'grinch trap.' I tied a string to the ceiling and attached a clothespin, a pencil, and a giant paperclip. As they marveled at this conglomeration hanging over their heads before our first test, I told my students about the grinches, which lived in our ceiling! These grinches, I explained, were hairy purple creatures that dropped into students' ears on quiz days, and caused them to make careless mistakes on assessments—even when they knew the material. Before every quiz, I would now set this trap, and the trap would now prevent them from being 'grinched'! The students stared at me in silent disbelief. Throughout the assessment, I could see them trying *not* to look up at that grinch trap. When the assessment concluded, I wondered if this off-the-wall effort would serve its purpose for my students—to make assessment more enjoyable, and to reduce careless mistakes. My effort accomplished its purpose so well, 'setting the trap' has become a ritual in my class, and I dare not give an exam without performing it! Students now look forward to assessment, and enjoy taking a test!

Another way to avoid the 'depressing assessing' attitude is to be sure you vary your assessment techniques. For example, do not always give quizzes. Some students are more performance-oriented. Allow them to create a model, demonstrate a concept, present orally, conduct an interview, make a video, or research the Internet. When you must test in the traditional manner, vary these methods as well. Multiple choice, true false, short essay, fill in the blank, and open response questions may be alternated or combined. This diversity not only eliminates the boredom of routine, it also assesses students multi-dimensionally and meets the multiple learning styles of your students. (See Appendix: *Addressing the Multiple Intelligences.*)

It is also important to help your students understand that assessment doesn't just evaluate them—it also helps you evaluate what *you* are doing to help *them*. Let your students know that assessment helps you become a better teacher. When middle schoolers understand that assessment helps everyone, it becomes less intimidating.

Middle schoolers love for you to read to them!

Most importantly, make sure your assessment is *authentic*. Authentic assessment has a real-world *purpose* and relates to the goals listed in your lesson. Authentic assessment does not test simply to be testing. Assessment must be (and be recognized by your students as) more than a mere regurgitation of facts. It must stimulate higher level thinking skills whenever possible and challenge your students to excel.

Second, however you choose to assess, it is important to provide your students feedback *immediately* and *often*. Students will learn more effectively when feedback is provided as near to the lesson learned as possible, and when they see it as a regular routine. It is especially effective in middle school to personalize feedback comments as often as you are able. Though time-consuming, there is powerful influence in a *personalized, positive* comment on a middle schooler's paper! Research has shown that grading which includes a teacher comment is up to three times more effective than grading alone. Then, return graded papers to students as soon as possible. Delayed feedback results in diminished effectiveness.

Finally, make your students understand that passing is the responsibility they must take. Provide every opportunity for your students to succeed. Address multiple intelligences and extol improvement, but resist the temptation to give what is not earned. Your students will learn neither responsibility nor the content through academic welfare.

The least I need to know: My to do checklist!

- ❏ I will remember in teaching my subject the difference between *nice to know* and *need to know.*
- ❏ I will be familiar with my subject core content, as well as state and national standards in my subject area.
- ❏ I will stay abreast of the latest research in my area.
- ❏ I will remember that scope and sequencing is a very effective organizational technique—both for me and for helping my students to learn.
- ❏ I will never forget that, in middle school, *relating* the material is the fundamental prerequisite for learning.
- ❏ I will remember that in teaching middle schoolers, *repetition* is never redundant.
- ❏ I will never forget that an ounce of need goes further than a pound of content.
- ❏ I will remember that *review* of material can take on many forms and that the more enjoyable the review is, the more effective will be the retention.
- ❏ I will practice asking my students more questions rather than merely feeding them information.
- ❏ I will vary my assessment techniques and never forget that middle schoolers vary not only in their learning styles, but also in the way they respond to differing assessment models.
- ❏ I will post my grading scale, and go over assessment procedures with my students *early*—and *often!*
- ❏ I will remember in assessment to praise *progress*, and understand that a little encouragement goes a long way.

6. Attitudes: *Building Atmosphere—*
creating a magical
environment!

Principle—"As a teacher, your job is not to fill a bucket, but to light a fire!"

Lesson I must learn: Your attitude toward your subject and your students is the most important key to student achievement. Your students will often learn more from the fire of your presentation than from the information in your lesson. Be excited! Enjoy what you do!

> ➤ Attitude Creates Atmosphere!
>
> ➤ The P.I.E. of Successful Teaching!
>
> ➤ Inviting Room or Grant's Tomb?
>
> ➤ Descending the ivory tower!

Attitude Creates Atmosphere!

The most important thing you will create in your classroom is not your perfect lesson plan, your reward system, or your wall décor. The most important thing you will create is the atmosphere of a learning environment where you and your students will spend the next nine months. Like it or not, your classroom will become a micro-family, with you as one parent and learning as the other. Classroom atmosphere will determine whether the learning experience is positive, negative, or exists at all, and the micro-family that is your classroom may well be a more inviting environment that many of your students' families at home. Be an inclusive teacher—toward *all* your students—not just the ones that are popular or make good grades. Make each one feel they have a purpose in your 'family'—let them play a part—even if they simply want to erase a board, or straighten your rows. The atmosphere your students perceive when they walk into your classroom will affect them, and the way they learn, the rest of the year.

One way to create a positive atmosphere in your classroom is to establish an *active* learning environment. The most negative learning environment you can create is to do nothing more than assign a task, threaten a test, discipline by the seat of your mood swing, and work at your desk until you are forced to get up and flick the light switch. A good teacher *engages* students, *establishes* behavior management, and *encourages* success!

Another way to create a positive classroom environment is to encourage your students to be respectful enough to use 'thank you' and 'please' in their conversations. Such courtesies not only foster positive personal habits, they also just make everyone *feel* more special!

A third way to create a positive atmosphere is to understand that a silent classroom doesn't always indicate a positive classroom environment. Sometimes it indicates diligent learning. At other times, it indicates fear.

Keep 'high walls,' 'small doors,' and 'wide yards' toward the students. Be sure they know you are in authority, but give them space to be creative and express themselves. Allow them a small but vital 'open spot' into discovering you, the teacher, as a real person. Never be afraid to try something new, silly, or 'on the spot.' The more they see your effort and 'humanness', the more respect you will earn. *"It's still true: they don't care how much you know until they know how much you care!"*

The *Pax Romana* was the 'peace of Rome.' It was a famous period known worldwide as a time of unparalleled splendor among the Emperors, and peace among the inhabitants. But the peace was an uneasy peace. Most parts of the empire did not challenge Rome due to fear, not due to satisfaction.

Mr. Steele was my science teacher in 7th grade. His classroom was so quiet visitors often thought he was on planning period. None of us dared talk without permission. This is nearly all I remember about Mr. Steele's class. This is not to say he was a poor teacher, or that quiet classrooms are not effective learning environments. But I never felt comfortable in an environment where I was silent out of fear. Before you assume that silence is always golden in a middle school classroom, be sure you understand that sometimes an active classroom is a classroom where students feel secure enough to discuss, while a quiet classroom sometimes indicates they are too afraid to care. Some students learn best through speaking, not merely listening. They are external thinkers whose voiced expression works for them as a personal review technique.

Attitude creates atmosphere. How you deal with diverse situations goes a long way in creating atmosphere in your classroom. Foster an attitude of *flexibility*. Understand that, by its very nature, middle school is a world of flux and change. Your perfect lesson plan will be interrupted. The student who most needs to stay in your room will be called to the office. The phone will ring in the middle of your best lesson. Also, foster an attitude *of patience*. Never overestimate how quickly your students learn, or underestimate how much even the most academically challenged students can grasp. Finally, foster a *sense of humor*. Don't take yourself too seriously. Relax a bit. If you blow it once and awhile, don't be afraid to laugh at yourself. Be silly in front of your students once and awhile. They will love to see this in you. Sometimes a sense of humor can save the day for you—and your students.

> **Fifty years from now it won't matter how rich you were or what car you drove. What will matter is that the world will be a better place because you were important in the life of a child.**

The P.I.E. of Successful Teaching!

Good teachers know how to combine three other ingredients to create a successful teaching atmosphere in a middle school classroom. Note that I didn't say a *survivable* atmosphere in a middle school classroom—you may survive without these—but these ingredients create a successful atmosphere. I call this my '*P. I. E. of successful teaching*'.

The *P* stands for *perseverance*.
The *I* stands for *inspiration*.
The *E* stands for *enthusiasm*.

Perseverance is the most important personal attitude you will develop as a teaching skill. Perseverance alone is what will get you through those inevitable times when your good lesson meets a bad day, and the whole thing flops. Try to remember that such days happen to all teachers, and that to simply persevere is often your only alternative. On other days, you will arrive late, inadvertently insult the secretary, embarrass the custodian, let a perfectly good teachable moment slip away, slip and fall on a wet spot where you mopped up vomit, forget your department meeting, and have the assistant principal spend two periods in your classroom observing your students forget every-

> **"Success is very often 20% aptitude, and 80% attitude."**

thing they learned yesterday! Remember too, that such days will always be balanced by days when the lesson you least expect will make an impression—succeeds! Never let discouragement build a nest in your self-confidence as a teacher. Push on through those days when you wonder if perhaps you should have gone into another profession. Hang in there! The most valuable lessons you never planned to teach your students might well be the patience, courage, and endurance you show under fire. Though you may not feel like it, smile, compliment, encourage. On those days when nothing seems to go right, remember—no matter how little you feel you have influenced a child's life— you *have* made an impression. *Persevere!*

Inspiration is the second piece of the pie of successful teaching. It is the most important attribute you can foster in your classroom! Let me say it one more time—inspiration is the most important attribute you can foster in your classroom. Remember, you will teach more effectively through *inspiration* than through *perspiration*. Middle schoolers are inspired by things they *enjoy*, things by which they are *challenged*, and adults who elicit *respect*. You will inspire your students to excel in each of these three ways.

Enthusiasm is the final slice of the pie. Enthusiasm is contagious. So is boredom.

I remember when I was in middle school, a few of my teachers seemed to have suffered from a 'charisma bypass'! They taught in 3-D: *dry, dull,* and *disjointed!* Not every teacher can have a magical personality. Every teacher can, however, inject some energy, courage to be creative, and enthusiasm into their lessons. Just as a yawn is picked up by others, so also is joy and excitement. Try teaching in a different 3-D: *dynamic*—put some enthusiasm into the lesson, *digestible*—break concepts down into smaller tidbits, and *developmentally appropriate*—remember, middle schoolers are still children. Amazingly, these attitudes do not always have to be *intentional* to be effective!

> A spoonful of sugar *still* helps the medicine go down! Whether reviewing or testing, if you can *make it fun*, students will be more productive...it's the nature of the 'beast'!

Middle schoolers are uniquely sensitive to tiny, often imperceptible cues we give them every day. A nod, a raised eyebrow, and a frown—all these convey a message. Studies have shown that students pick up on, and are affected by, most of these cues without ever realizing it! In a similar way, genuine enthusiasm becomes contagious in a middle school classroom, and students can become excited about learning whether they consciously choose to or not!

Your middle schoolers will come to you with some measure of enthusiasm. Much of what they bring will be due to individual personality. Unfortunately, much of what they've *lost* will be due to the classroom attitudes of their former teachers. In becoming a good teacher, learn how to build on what each student brings to you. Become enthusiastic about the job you do and the lessons you teach! As you do, you will watch your students become more receptive learners. *Channel* their enthusiasm, don't dam the flow! Relate to their interests! Remember, your students are people too.

> *Color, Creativity, and Caring* will take you further in middle school than just about anything else. Remember these '3 C's'. Kids *love* the first, *enjoy* the second, and *need* the third!

The '*P. I. E. of successful teaching.*' Perseverance, inspiration, and enthusiasm. Three vital ingredients for creating a successful teaching atmosphere in a middle school classroom, and instilling within your students the joy of learning!

Inviting Room or Grant's Tomb?

Walk into your classroom, and pretend you are seeing it for the first time through the eyes of a thirteen-year-old. What feeling does your room convey?

> Balance creativity with organization in your classroom. Don't be so creative that you're not organized, or so organized you're not creative.

What emotions does it evoke? Is your classroom clean, inviting, colorful, and (reasonably) organized? Or is it drab, dull, and more like a tomb than a room a middle schooler would enjoy spending seven per cent of his or her life in?

Your students will enjoy learning far more in a colorfully decorated classroom, and anything you can do to help students enjoy the learning process will be a large bonus in your favor! Take the time to decorate your room. Some research has shown that students tend to ask more questions in a colorful classroom. Put up some pictures and a colorful bulletin board. Put your name outside your door. Next to my door I have a small sign that reads, "*Through these doors pass the most important people in the world—my students!*" Also be aware of the lighting and *temperature* of your room. Small things such as these create an inviting atmosphere for young teens and get things off to a positive start *before* your students even walk through your door!

Also, display significant honors that you may earn. You are your students' teacher—they want to be proud of you! Your diploma was only the beginning. Let everyone who walks into your room know that you are proud of your profession and your accomplishments. Displaying your honors will not appear to your students as vanity on your part. It will give them a sense of pride that they've had a part in your success and in making you what you've become!

Descending the ivory tower!

Yes, you are a professional—never forget that. But you are also a teacher of middle schoolers—older *children*—never forget that either. Come down from the ivory tower of educational solemnity every once and awhile. Play with your students. Don't be so academically minded you become no classroom good!

Remember, those seats in your classroom are filled first by *children* who happen to be your students. They are children *first*, students second, and children need to be able to relax, at times, within a structured environment. Recognize when it's time to relax. Don't kill their hearts by pounding their heads! Core content is important, but 'core' alone is indigestible! Tell a story or two from when you were young. Never be afraid to laugh at yourself when the occasion warrants. Illustrate a point with a personal reference, and never forget that illustrations are windows to the mind—even for adults—*especially* for children. Some of my most effective lessons were illustrated by failures in my own life. Open up a little. Always remember—*you* are more important than what you *teach*, and some students will be motivated by the hero you have become in their eyes. Model effectively. Be a professional, but let the kids peak inside a bit.

> *Examples* are foundations in learning's temple, and *illustrations* are windows to the sanctuary! *"The average teacher TELLS. The good teacher EXPLAINS. The great teacher DEMONSTRATES. The master teacher INSPIRES!"*
>
> *(W. Ward)*

The least I need to know: My to do checklist!

❑ I will remember that, in the middle school classroom, *attitude* creates *atmosphere*, and that I have the ability to create or destroy an effective learning environment.

❑ I will understand that a quiet classroom may not indicate a successful learning environment, and that an active environment may not be indicative of ineffective behavior management.

❑ I will make my classroom an inviting place to enter.

❑ I will encourage *courtesy* in my classroom—and practice it myself.

❑ I will strive to be flexible, patient, and cultivate a sense of humor.

❑ I will endeavor to inspire my students to achieve, and never forget that my job is not to fill a bucket, but to light a fire!

❑ I will seek to enjoy what I do each day, and understand that enthusiasm is especially contagious in the middle school classroom.

❑ I will allow my students to get to know *me* a bit.

7. Strategies: *Building Learning— strategies that make it work!*

Principle—"Learning should be enjoyable! Make sure you don't kill their heart by pounding their head!"

Lesson I must learn: There is no perfect way to teach a lesson. It is the diversity in teaching strategies that make every classroom unique. However, a few strategies have stood the test of time, and are universally helpful in making students enjoy—not merely endure—the learning experience. Utilize and modify what has worked in the past to create new and innovative ways to teach your subject!

- ➢ *Numero Uno* on their list!
- ➢ Empowering your students—the fuel that runs their engines!
- ➢ The '5-10-15-20' rule!
- ➢ Teachable Moments
- ➢ Lay down a challenge!
- ➢ Cooperative Learning
- ➢ Shock their socks off!
- ➢ *'Dead Poets'* DO speak!

Numero Uno on their list!

What is the most important thing to middle schoolers? Is it their friends? Is it their clothes? Is it their reputations? Believe it or not, none of these is the most important thing. The most important thing to a teenager is their *name*, and the second most important thing is the work of their hands. Learn their names—their *preferred* names, and pronounce them correctly. This may seem a simple and non-vital function, but it is a powerful motivator. Keep a bulletin board to post student work or achievements. Be sure you have a place for student photos, which they will give you, and a place to display especially touching notes of appreciation. These show students you care about

Mood swings are rapid in middle schoolers!

them as individuals, and not merely as collection of students whom you must teach.

Empowering your students—the fuel that runs their engines!

Teenagers are often the very definition of chaos! They are random motion, jumbled emotions, predictable unpredictability, and organized confusion. They often seem to run on hormones and gum, and their engines sometimes seem to never run out of gas. The most effective fuel that runs a middle schooler's engine is not sugar, free time or hormones, however.

The fuel that runs their engine is the fuel that you as a teacher can give them with no fear of calorie counting, parent complaints, or lawsuits. The fuel that truly empowers a teenager is *encouragement*. Ninety-five percent of the individuals each of your students encounter on a school day will not offer them an encouraging word. Their fuel tank will run on low most of each day. Help fill their tank with encouragement. Encourage your students to be the very best they can be. Encourage them to do better on the next quiz, or during the next grading period. Be especially encouraging when a reticent student raises his or her hand to ask a question. Remember, they are taking a

> An ounce of *positive feedback* is worth more than a pound of criticism. Unfortunately, however, it won't be remembered nearly as long.

chance that the question might appear silly to their peers! Find something to praise in *every* question asked—even if it's just in the asking of it. Middle schoolers are highly impressionable when it comes to encouragement and discouragement. Foster the first. Eliminate the second.

The '5-10-15-20' rule!

Middle school is an environment where very young teenagers must sit for six or more hours in a structured environment, refocus at least that many times, and endure teachers of varying teaching abilities who love their subject infinitely more than the student does! Young teenagers are also social creatures, and are quick to accept compromises when they recognize they stand to gain. Remember the first. Channel the second. Life will be easier for everyone in your classroom.

One of my most successful time-management techniques is the '*5-10-15-20*' technique, which may be modified to suit any classroom. My students know that the first *five minutes* of class are theirs. They may socialize as long as I have no problem with volume. To keep this privilege, however, they understand that the next forty-five minutes are mine. Within that time block, *ten minutes* is for review time, where I assess prior knowledge through a questioning game, or 'oral quiz.' This is *feedback time* for me. The next *fifteen minutes* are for introducing new material, such as handouts or board work. Students learn the agenda (and the *purpose* for the agenda—*why* is always important in the learning process!), which I always post on an agenda board. I then set expectations by verbalizing expected outcomes, such as *"by the end of class..."*. This time is also used for review and re-focus, based upon previously learned material.

> **The spring season raises the 'sap', and drains the energy of a middle schooler. *Keep middle schoolers busy!***

The final *twenty minutes* is reserved for any combination of the following: discussion time, application and review of new material, small group or independent work, assigning and *practicing* tonight's homework (they should *always* begin homework in class!). This is followed by *closure*. Closure is your final summary of the completed lesson highlights. It impacts *retention* and makes *connections* to objectives.

The '*5-10-15-20*' technique allows students time to be social, but what is more important, it lets them know I understand their needs. It also shows them I care enough to allow them part ownership in our class time, but expect concerted, on-task diligence in return. Through a mere five minutes of compromise, I create an atmosphere of improved learning.

> **What you say during the *first and last* few minutes of a given class period will generally be what students are most likely to remember.**

The '*5-10-15-20*' technique also allows direct teaching time to be more inline with the attention-span of middle schoolers (generally twice their chronological age), and restricts *information overload*. Information overload is a detrimental—not just ineffective—teaching habit. It reduces comprehension, and is one of the biggest mistakes a new teacher can make. Information overload is the attempt to cover too much *information* in too short a *time*. When you find your students are starting lose focus, you need change course. You can always finish the lesson tomorrow. Remember, your goal is to teach your *students* your information—not just to teach the *information* to your students. Your job is to not merely to 'feed a head', but to *enrich a life!* Brevity is the key to dealing with middle schoolers. Maximize your point, and move on.

However you establish your time management policy, be sure you establish it as a classroom *routine!* Establish early—and remind often—your policies regarding pencil sharpening, copying assignments, bringing materials, etc. Middle schoolers thrive on procedure and consistency. Establish a channel of routine in your classroom, and the students will fill it.

Teachable Moments

The atmosphere you create in your classroom goes a long way in enhancing the learning environment for your students. The way you plan your lesson, the consistency with which you handle behavior, interruptions, etc., creates an atmosphere of safety and security. In such an atmosphere, middle schoolers thrive. There will be times, however, when the learning environment is improved—not reduced—by a spur-of-the-moment *change* on your part. That moment when a lesson plan is sacrificed for a more productive moment for learning. That occasion when fate unites an unexpected occasion with a hunger to know among your students, and an out-of-the-blue opportunity becomes more valuable than your finest lesson plan. Recognize these times when they occur, for they are a teacher's best friends. These are *teachable moments*, and they must be utilized to the fullest.

> Always save the fun stuff for *last*. Even the most dynamic personality can't compete with a puzzle!

My lesson was on the concept of democracy in ancient Greece. This was one of my favorite lessons, and I assumed the students would feel the same. I waxed eloquent on the privileges of free speech, rights of the individual, and the importance of the individual voice in the democratic process. My whole class was bored to tears, and many were put to sleep by my profound knowledge. I saw one of my best lessons sinking like the Titanic, when a thirteen-year-old suggested: *"How about letting us debate one of these?"* Not in the lesson plan, but that middle schooler brought to my attention the value of *'the teachable moment'*—that moment when the finest lesson plan must be tossed in order to capture the lesson in a way that one moment in time dictates.

Recognize genuine teachable moments. Do not confuse them with those 'divergent paths' that middle schoolers are so expert in leading teachers down. Teachable moments are rare and wonderful expeditions along a more creative road to learning. To utilize them, a good teacher cannot be afraid to sacrifice routine upon the altar of opportunity.

Lay Down a Challenge

Middle schoolers are experts in finding a point to disagree with. One of their favorite words is *'why?'* With high-strung middle schoolers, as with a river, it is generally easier to redirect the current than to dam the flow. Channel their innate inquisitiveness—do not stifle their creativity. Challenge them occasionally to disagree with a statement, and defend their position. State something as a rule, and middle schoolers will find an exception. Stimulate their thinking! Foster their innate curiosity! Play the devil's advocate to create controversy. Force them to think at a higher level.

> **An ounce of 'why' stimulates more learning than a pound of 'what'. However, 'why' is an unrecognized guest if 'what' doesn't answer the door.**

For example, in our philosophy unit, I had students defend (agree or disagree with) the statement: 'God cannot make a rock so big that even He can't move it.' Students immediately took sides and debated this philosophical dilemma. I followed up the activity with challenging open-response questions using *'why?' 'predict,'* and *'what if?'* prompts. Middle schoolers love a challenge. Use this to your teaching advantage.

Cooperative learning

Cooperative learning is a useful and effective strategy for learning. It is a learning strategy that is *not* easy to master. While cooperative learning has its place when effectively and sparingly used, too often it becomes an easy way to hope students are learning when a teacher has not spent the time necessary to prepare a lesson. Use cooperative learning *appropriately* when you use it. Keep your groups to three or four students. Establish a time limit and stick to it. Be sure to assign specific tasks in order to ensure involvement. Finally, require a product—make sure students know there was a purpose—and have them report group findings to the class. Cooperative learning only functions effectively when there are *expectations, procedures, responsibilities,* and *accountability*. Whenever you use this strategy, reserve time for whole-class discussion afterward.

Shock their socks off!

Interested in a strategy that will really make an impression on your students? Want to tell them some things they *never* thought they'd hear? Try this. When you make a mistake—any mistake—say to your students *"I'm sorry."* And when they ask you something about which you don't have a clue, say: *"I just don't know."* Middle schoolers think their teachers either know it all, or *think* they know it all. To admit you made a mistake, or that you don't know every answer, will not only endear you to your students, it will also teach them it's OK to sometimes not be perfect. They shouldn't expect you to be, and you won't expect it of them. Don't overdo this, but humble yourself a few times in front of the class, and your students will think *more* of you—not less.

'Dead Poets' DO speak!

Here's an activity that will pay lasting dividends in your classroom and allow you to relax without students while you learn it! It involves *teacher* homework, but you'll be a better teacher for the effort. Rent or purchase a copy of the 1987 Peter Weir film *Dead Poets Society*, starring Robin Williams. It's the story of an English teacher who doesn't quite fit into the conservative prep school where he teaches, but whose charisma and love of poetry inspire several boys. As you watch the film, write down every characteristic Williams exhibits that you feel makes him a memorable teacher. See how many of these strategies *you* might be able to adopt in your classroom. Remember, teachers who are remembered are teachers who leave a positive impression about learning, and isn't this why you entered this profession in the first place?

The least I need to know: My to do checklist!

- ❏ I will never put strict lesson planning ahead of teachable moments, and I will learn to recognize teachable moments whenever they come.
- ❏ I will remember that while cooperative learning has its place, I am the teacher and am paid to be the expert in my classroom.
- ❏ I will remember that the most important thing to my students is their name and seek to learn these quickly.
- ❏ I will cultivate encouragement in all my dealings with my students, for it is the fuel that runs their engines.

❑ I will challenge my students through higher level thinking skills.

❑ I will understand that middle schoolers are social creatures, and that allowing my students a bit of free time within a structured environment can create very effective leverage in encouraging them to use my time wisely.

❑ I will remember that if I don't *check* homework often, it will evolve into *no* home 'work' at all!

❑ I will remember that in teaching middle schoolers, it's easier for my lesson to run long, but *better* for it to go short!

❑ I will learn to apologize to my students when necessary, and to never be afraid to admit it when I just don't know an answer.

8. Teaming: *Building Unity—*
the sum is greater
than its parts!

Principle—"The broader the foundation, the taller the construction!"

Lesson I must learn: Working with other teachers in a team setting can greatly improve not only your effectiveness as a teacher, but also the ability of your students to broaden their learning experience. Use the leverage of interdisciplinary teaming to make your students multidimensional learners!

- ➤ Fitting In, and Firing Up!
- ➤ Together—we *can!*
- ➤ Teachers & kids are people too—*final thoughts*

Fitting In, and Firing Up!

If you are fortunate enough to be a part of a teaming environment, you have an opportunity to multiply your effectiveness in teaching your middle schoolers.

Teaming offers many benefits to you, but such benefits will require adjustments on your part. As a new teacher, you will face certain expectations in becoming a team player. Remember, fitting in with other team members is only the first step. Your main challenge in teaming is to fire up your students in a way that would not be possible in a non-teaming environment.

As the newest member of a middle school teaching team, your primary role is to fit *their* team. If you ever hope to elicit change, your team must see you as an integral part of the group—not as an intrusive faultfinder. This has been home to them, and you are coming in as the new roommate. To become a team player, help your team identify a common vision. Ask yourself where it is you want your team to go, and what do you want your team to accomplish?

The primary benefit of teaming is to help all team members learn the academic and affective strengths and weaknesses of your students. Groupings of students take on differing personalities and styles, and students perform differently in different environments, to be sure.

One year, our team had particular difficulty in dealing with a new group of 6th graders. Many team discussions took place regarding how we would manage them. Finally, the science teacher, while assigning projects, stumbled upon the answer to our dilemma. We had been attempting to control behavior by shutting it down. Through the projects created by the students, however, the science teacher discovered this group of students learned best through *expression* rather than restriction. We had been dealing with the students in exactly the *wrong* way. Because of the lack of control we perceived in other areas in which we dealt with the students, we had been afraid to encourage expression through activity. The science teacher, seeing the students in her environment, solved the dilemma for the entire team. Such is the strength of a teaming environment.

> **Some students actually will learn without notes...if *you're* good! Research has shown, however, that *note taking and summarizing* are two of the most powerful skills students can cultivate, and the more—the better.**

A second benefit of teaming is the teaching and reinforcement of social behavior. As a teacher, your job is not merely to teach your *subject* to your students. Your job is to teach your *students* your subject, and, what is more important, how to become well-rounded contributors to our society. Teaming allows you to share with—and learn from—experienced teachers on handling and shaping behaviors as your students move through diverse settings.

A third benefit of teaming is the ability to employ consistency in team policies, which may, or may not, differ from regular school policies. These policies might include how your team decides to deal with discipline, homework, field trips, newsletters, parent meetings, social activities, and block scheduling. Remember, consistency is king in the middle school environment.

> **Remember—more often than not— middle schoolers really don't like themselves. They are quite sensitive, and even casual teasing can be hurtful.**

A fourth benefit of teaming is the ability to employ cross-curricular instruction. Middle schoolers learn more efficiently when similar material is taught in different classes. The ability to present differing aspects of common themes greatly enhances diversity in student development and adds a multi-dimensional flavor to what it is we want middle schoolers to learn. This allows students to *generalize* and *apply* information.

A fifth benefit of teaming is the recognition that every child has a different personality, temperament, and disposition. Teaming allows students to relate to particular teachers with similar personalities, or experiences, and learn to accept other teachers whose personalities they may not so easily relate to. In this way, students learn to deal more effectively with the real-world environment they will face.

Teaming is more than merely division of responsibility—it is multiplication of opportunity! It is the pooling of expert knowledge across a middle school curriculum, and provides for your students a unity within a diverse atmosphere, which *is* a middle school.

Together—we can!

If you are part of a team, you are part of a sharing environment. Your input becomes an integral part of the group personality. As part of a team, your contribution shapes the decision-making process, and the sum is free to become greater than the individual parts.

Research has shown that successful student learning takes place by the extent to which teachers *plan* together, *discipline* in consistency and unity, and *problem-solve* together. Planning is the key. *Goals* are the essence. *Flexibility* is the requirement.

Without a shared vision, strife may divide team members, and goals may not be realized. Teams function best as a symphonic unit, whose instruments must be played in harmony. Important questions for successful teaming include:

- What are we trying to teach?
- How are we going to achieve our goals?
- How will we recognize if we are being successful?
- What role does each member play in the process?
- How will we evaluate success?
- Is each subject area represented in the endeavor?
- Is it *necessary* for each subject area to participate?

If your students perceive you and your colleagues as a team, and the unit as important, they will buy into the process.

Teachers & kids are people too—*final thoughts*

Your room is prepared. Your energy—piqued. That first lesson of the year is begging to be taught, and you are excited about having a wonderful year!

Though you will make more than your share of mistakes this first year, with experience you will undoubtedly become an excellent teacher. Just remember—such excellence does not come quickly, and the road to reaching it is often paved with a few rough spots along the way. Learn to distinguish between the things you can change and learn from, and the things over which you have no control.

One thing over which you may have little or no control is how other teachers respond to you. Of course, you should do everything you can to earn the respect of your colleagues *(Chapter 4)*. This means you will sometimes need to apologize when you are wrong, and practice a little humility when you are right. But just as you will unavoidably have personality conflicts with certain students you teach, so also, you will find that not all your colleagues will warm up to you as you might hope. Teachers are people too, remember, and personality conflicts are just a fact of life in every profession.

Don't be discouraged when some colleagues find fault with you when you've done your best, or when another teacher is not as skilled in apologies as you are. Don't take it personally when another teacher seems to enjoy disagreeing with you at every opportunity. Remember, your job is first to shape the lives of young people, and that should be the thing that concerns you most. Let go of the things you can't control, and be the best teacher you can be.

> **Never sacrifice the teaching of fundamental information on the altar of cooperative learning. Hands-on is very important, but what they *enjoy* must not substitute for what they *need*. They may learn from each other, but *you* are the teacher!**

Finally, never forget—you are there to teach your students *first*, and your subject, second. While core content and assessment are the essence of what you are being paid to teach, they are not *all* you do. You are in the life-shaping profession, and, as a middle school teacher, your influence is especially vital. While even your best lessons may not be remembered in a year, *you* will be. And not just for one year, but for the rest of the lives of your students. Your students will remember far longer—your encouragement, those endearing spontaneous moments, how you signed a yearbook or dried a tear, and how you shaped their lives by your influence, by being the person you were—than they will the information you taught. Be the best teacher you can be—not by filling a brain, but by shaping a life!

The least I need to know: My to do checklist!

- ❏ I will remember that I am a part of a team, and that my input is a valuable contribution to the group, as well as to student learning.
- ❏ I will remember that I need to fit in with the team, and value the contributions of the other members as much as I would want my input to be valued.
- ❏ I will remember that compromise is necessary to teaming successfully.
- ❏ I will remember that no matter what I do, I won't be able to please everyone I work with.
- ❏ I will remember that I teach so much more than information, and that teachers really *do* change lives.

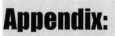

Appendix:

Handouts and Supplementary helps

When conferencing with parents:

✓ Meet parents at the door.

✓ *Document everything!*

✓ Arrange the conference setting so parents do not feel on the spot, or 'us against them.'

✓ Remember, parents are usually more nervous about conferences than you are.

✓ Start and end with something positive.

✓ Invite both parents where this is possible.

✓ Check with your guidance office before discussing the student with non-custodial parents, stepparents, etc. Such may not have rights to privacy.

✓ Keep a written record of the conference and give one copy to the parents.

✓ Do not schedule a conference that will have to be rushed through. Allow adequate time.

✓ Anticipate questions and have documented records of grades, conduct reports, sample work, etc.

✓ Address parents by name, and be sure you have the correct pronunciation.

✓ Don't assume every student has the typical nuclear family. Anticipate surprises.

✓ Listen to what the parent has to say—really *listen*, and look them in the eye.

✓ Ask if possibly there are extenuating circumstances, which might be affecting the child.

✓ Focus on solutions rather than emphasizing the problem.

✓ Schedule a future conference if necessary. Arrange for some type of follow-up.

✓ Deal in specifics. Do not drown parents in vague generalities. That is not why they came.

✓ Seek the parents' help in helping their child. Present yourself as an ally—not a foe.

✓ Focus on strengths as well as weaknesses. Every child has both.

✓ Do not work on other things in the presence of a parent. Appear as though the conference is as important to you as it obviously is to them.

✓ Speak in parent language—not educational techno-jargon. Parents will not be impressed.

How to survive opening day!

- ☐ Arrive early.
- ☐ Smile.
- ☐ Set your clock and watch to the bell schedule!
- ☐ Does my room appear colorful, challenging, and inviting through the eyes of a thirteen-year-old who must spend a year of his/her life in it?
- ☐ Do I have a temporary seating chart?
- ☐ Do I have a prepared lesson for day one?
- ☐ Do I have a plan for homeroom forms, locker assignments, etc.?
- ☐ Do I have an emergency lesson for a sub or myself?
- ☐ Do I have a first day gum, bathroom, and tardy policy prepared?
- ☐ Do I have an inviting sign outside my door with my name, subject, and grade?
- ☐ Do I have something I want to be remembered as the first thing I want to say?
- ☐ Do I understand that 70% of the impression I will make is made on the first day?
- ☐ Do I have my name written on the board?
- ☐ Do I have an adequate supply of board markers and erasers?
- ☐ Am I fully cognizant of my district and school rules, policies, and procedures?
- ☐ Do I have a list of supplies I want my students to bring to class daily?
- ☐ Do I have a prepared cafeteria expectation policy for my lunch group?
- ☐ Do I know my table assignment in the cafeteria at lunch?
- ☐ Do I understand the first day's schedule for classes, lunch, and absentee reporting?
- ☐ Do I have my room rules condensed down to the top five and have them posted?
- ☐ Do I have my first week's lesson plans completed and available?
- ☐ Do I have a seating chart plan?
- ☐ Am I aware of the special education and gifted students whose needs I also have to meet?

- ❏ Am I aware of any health concerns or medication requirements my students may have?
- ❏ Do I have (or want) an icebreaker activity planned?
- ❏ Do I have individual class schedules ready for each student?
- ❏ Do I have a posted emergency escape plan for fire and severe weather?
- ❏ Do I have a list of important phone numbers that I can find quickly?
- ❏ Do I have my temporary class roster, and have I gone over name pronunciation?
- ❏ Do I have a locker assignment plan?
- ❏ Do I have a planning book, grade book, and personal appointment calendar or organizer?
- ❏ Do I have a lunch ticket plan?
- ❏ Do I have a plan for any monies collected?
- ❏ Do I have enough books?
- ❏ Do I have enough desks?
- ❏ Do I have a course syllabus prepared for each student?
- ❏ Am I prepared for *Murphy's Law?*
- ❏ Do I have a prepared policy for student telephone use, loaning lunch money, etc.?

Room essentials to remember!

- ☐ A box of *Band Aids*
- ☐ Bottle of multi-purpose contact solution
- ☐ A can of air freshener
- ☐ A can of disinfectant
- ☐ A can of *Oops* or similar cleaners for emergencies
- ☐ Paper towels
- ☐ A canister for lost and used pencils
- ☐ A comfortable stool
- ☐ A small locker mirror attached to a wall or board
- ☐ A working pencil sharpener (don't forget to empty it daily!)
- ☐ A working stapler (remember to refill it!)
- ☐ A good supply of *Post-it* Notes
- ☐ A pop-up container of *Handi-wipes*
- ☐ A small portable erasable white board
- ☐ Assignment & Homework schedule 'due board'
- ☐ Posted bell schedule *with Lunch!*
- ☐ Boxes of *Kleenex*
- ☐ Calendar
- ☐ Waste basket (or two!)
- ☐ Clock (*behind* students if possible)
- ☐ Display board for student pictures/work
- ☐ Emergency exit diagram
- ☐ Emergency lesson plan (for anyone to teach)
- ☐ Emergency/School phone number list
- ☐ Room hall pass or sign-out sheet
- ☐ School Grading Scale
- ☐ Scotch tape dispenser
- ☐ Sub folder
- ☐ Sufficient board markers/chalk, with erasers

Addressing the Multiple Intelligences

Linguistic/Verbal (Attorneys, Authors, Ministers, Sales!)
"Just give me the words, man—I think in words!"

Involve creative reading, writing, and storytelling!
Share ideas
Debate an issue
Assign a presentation
Emphasize vocabulary terms
Study etymology
Use flash cards
Use word association and Jeopardy-type games
Utilize puns, similes, metaphors, and limericks

Spatial/Visual (Artists, Interior decorators, Architects, Photographers!)
"If I can see it, I can…"

Make a collage
Create a brochure
Design a poster
Emphasize color and perspective
Use pictures and photos
Show videos
Involve a chart or map
Utilize their imagination
Illustrate a story
Use diagramming and visualization scenarios

Logical/Mathematical (Accountants, Scientists, Computer programmers, Detectives!)
"I think in the abstract, and I'm a problem-solver!"

Perform experiments
Design a graph or timeline
Use a calculator
Utilize prediction

Evaluate an idea, decision, video, or book
Utilize compare and contrast
Solve a dilemma
Create a code or symbol activity
Use syllogisms and analogies
Interpret data
Utilize prediction of consequences
Design a puzzle

Musical/Rhythmic (Musicians, Composers!)
"If I can hear it, I can…"

Sing a song
Write a jingle
Research a Rocker!
Analyze a commercial
Play background music
Utilize videotaping and multimedia opportunities

Interpersonal (Politicians, Teachers, Actors!)
"Let's do it together!"

Have group presentations
Debate in pairs
Make rows into teams!
Role-play!
Present group problem-solving activities
Emphasize taking turns
Establish group goals
Utilize E-mail and telephone activities
Conduct interviews and surveys!
Let students teach!
Use cooperative learning and partnering paradigms

Intrapersonal *(Theologians, Philosophers, Psychologists!)*
"Can I just think about this awhile?"

Assign a journal
Allow sustained silent reading
Assign an opinion paper
Reflect and write about issues and events
Assign individualized projects and independent study
Have students personalize assignments, scenarios, events, etc.
Do self-study quizzes and inventories

Bodily/Kinesthetic *(Athletes, Surgeons, Dancers, Carpenters!)*
"Let's get down and DO it, baby!"

Play a charade or pantomime game
Involve an outdoor activity
Perform a play
Role-play an event
Assign a project or experiment
Relate learning to sports
Take field trips
Work with manipulatives

Naturalistic *(Ecologists, Zoologists!)*
"If we can GO, I'll GROW!"

Take a field trip
Involve outdoor activities
Utilize pictures and photos
Go on a hike
Have students sort, categorize and classify
Use collection, organization, and reporting activities

Important documents to keep!

- ❑ A current copy of your teaching certificate and school district contract
- ❑ A current list of any professional development you've earned (dated and described)
- ❑ A list of your core content or National/State Standards in your subject area
- ❑ Copies of all your past and current teaching evaluations/observations
- ❑ Copies of any honors, commendations, and accomplishments
- ❑ Current salary schedule
- ❑ Letters from parents, the community, and significant notes from students
- ❑ Summary notes from parent conferences or administrator conferences
- ❑ The school, school board, or county employee policy manual or code of ethics
- ❑ Parent contact forms
- ❑ Field trip forms
- ❑ Copy of conduct or discipline reports filed

Chicken Soup for Parenting: *"HELP! I woke up and my child was a 7th grader!"*

Dear Mom and Dad: the bad news is—*you* have to survive middle school *too!* The good news is—here are some research-based and imminently practical suggestions to make sure your middle schooler is successful. Employ (and *enjoy!*) each of these *"Dare to Care"* help tips written specifically for *you*—the parents of a middle schooler. Remember—when you help your child, you are helping your child's teacher also!

> *"The job of a teacher is not to fill a bucket, but to light a fire."*

Utilize Schoolnotes.com to find out what we're doing, and note other helpful links (references, homework helps, daily activities, extra credit, etc.) for both you and your child. I keep my website up to date and have one of the highest 'visit' totals in Kentucky. Don't have a computer? Your child may call a friend on any extra credit assignment. *Schoolnotes works!*

PLEASE.... PLEASE.... PLEASE **check agenda books and notebooks** daily, and **please check your child's grades!** It has been my experience that if he or she cannot show their grades to you, *90% of the time they are failing social studies.* All grades and graded papers are kept in these two books. **PLEASE help me help them**—check daily! Find playful ways to check up on assignments. Do a few problems together, show them how to correct mistakes, and then *let your child work alone.* Even if you feel you can't help with homework—if nothing else—you can help with organization skills, which will eventually help everything else!

Homework. Research has shown that **ten minutes per night multiplied by the grade level** is the most efficient (total) time to be allotted for homework. Help set up a consistent, organized *schedule* and *place* for homework to be done—with supplies and good lighting. Middle Schoolers thrive on routine. Help establish one. (*Homework is independent, unmonitored practice!*)

Also regarding homework, if your child is practicing a *skill*, ask him/her to tell you what's easy, what's hard, and **how they are** *going to improve.* If your child is doing a *project*, ask them **what knowledge they are** *applying* in the project. If they cannot answer these questions, the homework is useless—something is wrong—and you probably need to find out what it is.

Homework should be considered a 'quiet time' in which you are available to help. Nevertheless, when bedtime comes, stop your child from homework—even if the homework is not done. Sufficient sleep takes a backseat only to nutrition & nurture in importance for growth in teens. *Suggestion:* **Have them set out all books and papers the night before,** so they won't be rushed into forgetting things in the morning.

Whenever possible, **connect homework to family activities** (math to pricing items, social studies to upcoming TV documentaries and family trips, language arts to films, newspaper and magazine readings, etc.) *This increases the quality of learning logarithmically!*

Reward positive accomplishments (an agenda book completely filled in, perfect papers, etc.) on a *weekly* basis. **An ounce of** *positive feedback* **is worth more than a pound of criticism.** (Unfortunately, however, it won't be remembered nearly as long.) A little goes a long way, and middle schoolers love routine.

Keep a scrapbook or memory box of their middle school years. **Your child really will look back upon these years as the most special.** By the time high school rolls around, the opportunity to create something so sweet will be gone forever.

Ask your child to teach you at least three new things they learned each day! *Listening* is one of the greatest—and most neglected—skills of parenting. Discuss daily school activities each evening! **Look your child in the eye and** *really* **listen!**

Plan at least one visit to *each* of your child's classes during the year, and attend school functions as often as you are able. While you may not be able to attend every school function—as a general rule—*parents who care are parents who are there!*

Be tolerant of a low score every once in a while, but never, *never* **accept a 'zero'** without finding out why. We all have off days, but a zero is either a careless attitude or a lesson unlearned, and both are disastrous to academic averages and character development!

Be a parent—not a friend. Lay down firm rules and consequences at home, and hold your child accountable. At first they'll complain, soon they'll appreciate it, and when they mature, they will thank you for the rest of their lives. ***Remember—even though you can't be a perfect parent, you can still be a good one.*** **"Dare to Care!"**

Please feel free to contact me through any of these web addresses:

My *Georgetown Middle School* email: jparks@scott.k12.ky.us

My **Personal email:** kidztchr7@hotmail.com

My *Schoolnotes.com* **site:** http://www.schoolnotes.com/40324/jparks.html

Writing a Feature Article
Lesson Plans
"The Democratic Process and the Freedoms We Enjoy"
(As a required portfolio writing entry)

Created by: Jerry L. Parks, Social Studies-7,
Georgetown Middle School, Georgetown, KY

Grade level: 7

Subject: Social Studies

Overview:

Students will understand how the democratic process is a foundational concept in America and how our representative form of government is a by-product of the search for freedom. *Academic Expectations: 2.14, 2.15, 2.16, and 2.19*

Skill:

Students will learn how one patriot, Jessica Lynch, changed her perception of the freedoms we enjoy due to her service in Iraq, and how to formulate their own feature article (portfolio piece) based upon this exemplar. *Academic Expectations: 2.14, 2.15, 2.16, and 2.17*

Assignment:

Students will write a feature article on *"Why I'm glad I'm an American"*

Expectations:

Students will better understand the cost of freedom, and the Pledge to our flag.

Materials needed:

1. Article on the pledge of allegiance by Jessica Lynch
2. Pencil and paper for students

Room modifications or equipment needed:

None

Time Allotment:

2-3 class periods

Terms/Concepts to Learn or Review:

Democracy
Republic
Dictatorship
Monarchy
Allegiance
Indivisible

Homework to Assign:

Students will complete the task by tomorrow.

Preparation and Standards Addressed:

1. Students will understand the concept of democracy.
2. Students will understand the concept of representative government and how it differs from democracy.
3. Students will have studied the contrast between these government forms and the dynastic dictatorships of ancient Egypt and kingships of Sumer.
4. Students will be familiar with, and experienced in, composing a (required) portfolio entry.
5. Students will be familiar with the pledge of allegiance to our flag.

Activity:

Discuss with students the requirement of portfolio entries from social studies.

Discuss with students the pledge of allegiance and Jessica Lynch.

Discuss with students the importance of freedom and the democratic process.

Read Jessica Lynch's *"What the Pledge Means to Me"(Parade,* 11/16/03).

Discuss with students the thoughts stimulated by the article and have them brainstorm possible inclusions for the article, such as *democracy, freedoms, worship, equality, responsibilities, rights, capitalism,* etc.

Challenge students to understand the concept of a feature article (stressing *audience,* etc.).

Discuss and begin the assignment (writing a feature article), which should be completed as homework.

Students should begin the process in class and be directed and redirected as necessary.

Follow-up activity:

Students discuss the feature-writing process and differing views on why each chose the subject they chose. *Academic Expectations: 2.14, 2.15, 2.16, and 2.17*

Students will be given the opportunity to share their feature article with the class and stimulate discussion on what made each a successful writing piece.

Review for Emphasis:

Discuss with the students how and why different cultures around the world have differing views of freedom, why the democratic process allows the most benefit to the citizen, and the responsibilities and sacrifices necessary to maintain such a culture. *Academic Expectations: 2.14, 2.15, and 2.16*

Evaluation & Assessment:

(Students will be evaluated according to a teacher-created rubric.)

Parent Alert Notification

Social Studies-7
Jerry Parks, Instructor

Dear Parent/Guardian:
I need your help. This form is being sent to you to alert you that your son/daughter is experiencing a serious difficulty in Social Studies. Any assistance on your part would be most helpful. Please feel free to contact me if you would like to discuss this matter, *or send feedback on the other side of this form, and return it to me.*

Student: _____ Date: _____

Current Social Studies Grade: Conduct: *Excellent* _____
A B C D F   *Satisfactory* _____
                                                                      Unsatisfactory _____

| The problem at this time is regarding: |

Low Test Scores _____

Failure to Turn in Assignments _____

Unexplained Drop in Work Quality _____

Inappropriate Talking or Language _____

Appears Unmotivated, Unconcerned _____

Seems to Not Understand; Confused & Off-task _____

Discipline Problem/Refusal to Cooperate _____

Explanation: _____

_____

_____

Thank you very much for your concern and assistance in this matter. Our goal is for all students to reach their maximum level of achievement, and I knew you'd want to know about this problem before final grades make it too late to change.

Jerry L. Parks,
Georgetown, Middle School

Parent signature_____

How you can be reached: _____

Bloom's Taxonomy

Level I: Knowledge—to learn and bring to mind information.

Memory recall of basic facts and answers.
Prompts: *who, what, list, find, match, define, where, label, name, show, recall, omit, count, locate, trace, underline, record, pick, quote, choose, fill-in, identify, tell, match*

Important for foundational support.
Developed through practice and repetition.

❑ The student absorbs, remembers recognizes, and responds.

"Where are pyramids located?"

Demonstrators: vocabulary lists, workbook activities, quizzes

Level II: Comprehension—to understand and grasp the meaning of information.

Demonstration of facts by interpretation (meaning) or description.
Prompts: *rephrase, compare, contrast, explain why, summarize, illustrate, outline, show, associate, describe, define, reword, simplify, exemplify, change, interpret*

Requires an extension of knowledge, or basic use of an idea.
Directed toward a specific *action* or *communication*.

❑ The student translates or interprets, but does not relate information to other material.

"Contrast the differences between Egyptian and Mesoamerican pyramids."

Demonstrators: drawings, diagrams

Level III: Application—to use learned material in a new and specific situation.

Problem-solving by transferring and applying previous information to that which is new or different.
Prompts: *apply, utilize, choose, interview, solve, model, for example, develop, organize, predict, identify, determine, modify, if, utilize, transfer, suppose, participate, distinguish, derive*

> Requires not merely use of learned material, but use in a new way.
> Implies a transfer of training.
> Learner must recognize a problem and decide from given choices what will solve it.

> ❑ The student solves or constructs in new situations using principles, concepts, or theories.

> *"Give an example of modern technology that might have made pyramid building easier in the ancient world."*

> *Demonstrators:* Recipes, models, artwork,
> demonstration

Level IV: Analysis—to break down info in order to understand organizational structure.

Examining and breaking down information to identify cause. Infer and support generalizations produced.
Prompts: *analyze, infer, categorize, simplify, conclude, examine, assume, relate, justify, criticize, detect, diagram, when would, discriminate, transform, sort, survey, group, inspect, dissect, differentiate, specify*

> Requires the learner to: 'read between the lines,' find subtle cues, and study organization patterns.

> ❑ The student divides information into component elements.

> *"In your opinion, why do cultures feel the need to build such great structures?"*

> *Demonstrators:* Advanced writing and reasoning expression

Level V: Synthesis—to reformulate the component parts together into a new whole.

Compiling and combining elements in a new pattern, or propose alternative solutions.
Prompts: *estimate, construct, imagine, compose, solve, improve, propose how, design, arrange, extend, devise, formulate, integrate, suppose, revise, pretend, invent, predict*

> Involves careful thought of a previous creation.
> Requires the reverse intellectual process from analysis.
> Learner recognizes a problem and proposes ideas or material, which will solve it.
>
> ❑ The student reforms a (new) whole and can apply and analyze it.
>
> *"Pretend you were spending one day in either ancient pyramid-building culture. Write one entry in your journal on your feelings as you watched the ancient pyramid builders at work."*
>
> *Demonstrators:* Inventions, lesson plans, songs, poems, advertisements

Level VI: Evaluation—to judge the value of info against criteria for a given purpose.

Reflecting on and making recommendations of material.
Prompts: *appraise, argue, critique, test, verify, validate, interpret, measure, evaluate, defend, support, recommend, rank, grade, judge whether, determine, justify, assess, prioritize*

> Learner judges through careful thought and application of a criteria, which they generate and justify, as relevant.
>
> ❑ The student determines value according to purpose and against a criterion.
>
> *"Should the ancient pyramids be preserved as tourist attractions, or removed for land reclamation and farming? Justify your position."*
>
> *Demonstrators:* Editorials, critiques, rating
> scales, debates

Note: Research has shown consistently that students who can *analyze, synthesize,* and *evaluate* become more effective thinkers.

Parks' Ponderables

I.   Life isn't fair. Get used to it.

II.   The real world won't care about you nearly as much as we do right now. Appreciate it. Don't cop an attitude.

III.   If you think teachers are tough, wait till you get a boss someday!

IV.   Don't blame others for your mistakes. Taking more responsibility makes you look less like a child.

V.   Teachers are not responsible for ensuring that you have fun. They *are* responsible to make sure you learn. Don't complain. There are worse places you could be.

VI.   Your reputation is your most important possession. Cheaters are losers—remember that.

VII. TV bears no resemblance to the real world. Don't think that life will always entertain you, or that its problems are neatly resolved in half hour segments.

VIII. How you speak and present yourself is the *first* impression you will make on others. If you do it poorly, it may also be the *last* impression you make on a prospective employer when you interview someday.

IX.   Things are not true because we tell you, we tell you because they're true. Trust us—we have your best interest at heart.

X.   You generally receive the same respect you give, so use your brain before you exercise your mouth.

XI.   Life isn't divided into grading periods, nor does it give you summers off. Stop complaining about school and enjoy the ride while you can.

XII.   Take advantage of opportunities. Some, you will only get once.

XIII.   Unlike school, life doesn't give you as many chances as you need to get everything right. *Think* before you do or say something that might affect the rest of your life.

XIV.   Honor your parents and strive to be *better* than they are. They brought you up. Don't let them down.

XV.   Never put off till tomorrow what *needs* to be done today.

XVI.   Control what you say. Remember you can't *un-say* something, so don't use extreme words like *love* and *hate* without meaning them.

GEORGETOWN MIDDLE SCHOOL
730 North Hamilton Avenue
Georgetown, Kentucky 40316

Dear Parent:

I know you are always getting letters from teachers when your child is doing poorly in school, so it is with great pleasure that I write to tell you…this *isn't* the case! This is a letter of <u>appreciation</u> that is overdue and most deserved!

Some students make the teaching profession not only easy, but also enjoyable in so many ways. Jared is one of those students. The first half of our year is soon to be over, and sometimes we forget to pay compliments where they are most deserved. Kids like Jared are generally the exception in middle school (rather than the rule), and I didn't want to be remiss in telling you how fortunate I feel.

Jared really *is* a teacher's 'dream' to be able to teach. Pretty good grades, seldom a discipline problem, conscientious about keeping up, a pleasant and cooperative attitude—Jared *is* all of these! (You probably think I got the wrong address, right?!) Truthfully, to have a full class of students like this would be as rewarding as it would be impossible; nevertheless, I wanted to say thanks!

If you'd ever like to just drop in sometime, feel free. The kids love to show what they know when visitors come by! It is a joy and a privilege to be able to teach social studies to Jared. Upbringing shows in our classrooms, and this case is no exception.

Just thought you'd like to know.

Very sincerely,

Jerry Parks
Social Studies Department Chair
Georgetown Middle School

Great websites for teachers!

The following websites offer every imaginable type of help to teachers across the curriculum. Sites include lesson planning, resume writing, student homework helps, homework posting sites, free material for teachers, humorous quotes and sayings, clipart for all purposes, brain challenges, photo posting, puzzle-makers, online quiz taking, etc.

http://abcteach.com/
http://ask.com/
http://atozteacherstuff.com/
http://homeworkspot.com/middle/
http://members.aol.com/donnandlee/index.html
http://middleschoolhub.org/school/school.cfm
http://puzzlemaker.school.discovery.com/
http://quizstar.4teachers.org/indexi.jsp
http://resumes-for-teachers.com/
http://sitesforteachers.com/index.html
http://teachingtreasures.com.au/
http://w.webring.com/hub?ring=k12resource
http://www.braingle.com/
http://www.creativeteachingsite.com/
http://www.edhelper.com/
http://www.etymonline.com/
http://www.freakyfreddies.com/teacher.htm
http://www.iloveschools.com/
http://www.inspiringteachers.com/
http://www.justfreestuff.com/teacher.html
http://www.lessonplansearch.com/
http://www.lessonplanspage.com/
http://www.middleweb.com/Homework.html
http://www.nytimes.com/learning/teachers/index.html
http://www.ofoto.com/Welcome.jsp
http://www.parent.net/homework/index.shtml
http://www.puzzledepot.com/cwe/index.shtml
http://www.quotesandsayings.com/
http://www.refdesk.com/homework.html#jrhi
http://www.school-clip-art.com/
http://www.schoolexpress.com/

http://www.schoolnotes.com/40324/jparks.html
http://www.schoolpak.com/homework.htm
http://www.teacherhumor.com/
http://www.teacherplanet.com/calendar/0604.html
http://www.theteacherscorner.net/
http://www.timesaversforteachers.com/

The 'Mastery Principle' of a Successful Lesson Plan!

Here is everything college, experience, and professional development can teach you about teaching, condensed into seven simple tidbits! Fine tune, practice, and perfect these, and you will be the best teacher you can be. **Make sure your lessons are:**

M—*multiple intelligences addressed.* Does my lesson create a broad opportunity for learning by recognizing and addressing the diversity of learning styles among my students?

A—*application centered.* Does my lesson provide for my students to be able to apply the learning to their personal, social, cultural, or global concerns?

S—*standards based.* Does my lesson stem from the state and national standards in my subject area and cover the content I am supposed to be teaching?

T—*testing and assessment geared.* Does my lesson link into a measurable, valid, and cumulative assessment for my students to demonstrate what they have learned in a variety of ways?

E—*engagingly presented.* Does my lesson capture the interest of my students and challenge them into forced questioning, goal setting, and critical thinking skills?

R—*resource friendly.* Does my lesson utilize diverse resource materials extending beyond the textbook, such as other people, interdisciplinary units, activities, technology, the community, and practical lessons from everyday life?

Y—*youth focused.* Does my lesson focus first on the needs of my students—considering their age, prior knowledge, and experiences? Does the lesson allow more for student investigation rather than merely being teacher—practical?

'Time Capsule'

"Back to the Future!"
(Can your perceptions change?)

Your name _____ Today's Date _____

Right now, who are your two _best_ friends?

_____

What is one book you'd like to read, but haven't?

_____

What do you think will be your _hardest_ class at GMS this year?

_____

What are some popular movies, songs or video games out right now?

_____

_____

Who is one person you *just don't like*?

_____

What do you predict will be the _highest_ and _lowest_ grade you will make in social studies for any nine-week grading period?

_____

Which unit in social studies do you think you will like _most_ (Mesopotamia, Egypt, The Hebrews, Greece, Rome)?

_____

What is one 'wish' that you hope *comes true* for you in your life during this school year?

_____

_____

IF YOU COULD GO OUT WITH ANY TWO OR THREE GUYS/GIRLS IN
SCOTT COUNTY THIS YEAR, WHO WOULD THEY BE?

IMPORTANT!! This time capsule is not to be opened until Mr. Parks' social
studies classes open all of them in *May, 2005!*

"The Teacher's Ten Most Effective Words"

1.   *Thanks!*

2.   *I apologize…*

3.   *Quite an improvement!*

4.   *I'm proud of you!*

5.   *I've noticed the hard work!*

6.   *You help make my job fun!*

7.   *I'm fortunate to have YOU in class!*

8.   *I'll bet they're proud of you at home!*

9.   *Could you help me teach this a little better?*

10.   *I know it's difficult, but together we can do it!*

References for suggested reading

Bloom, B.S., Engelhart, M.D., Furst, E.J., Hill, W.H., & Kratwohl, D.R. (1956). *Taxonomy of Educational Objectives: Cognitive Domain, Handbook 1.* New York: David McKay.

Gardner, H., (1999). *Intelligence Re-framed: Multiple Intelligences for the 21st Century.* New York: Basic Books

Heidemann, S., & Hewitt, D. (1992). *Pathways to Play.* St. Paul, MN: Redleaf Press.

Marzano, Robert, Pickering, Deborah, Pollock, Jane, (2001). *Classroom Instruction that Works.* Alexandria, VA: ASCD Publications.

Scavone, Natalie, (2003). *National Board Certification: A Journey of Professional Development.* Chicago, IL: Robin Fogarty & Associates.

Steffy, Wolfe, Pasch & Enz (1999). *Lifecycle of the Career Teacher.* Corwin Press.

Wilkinson, Bruce, (1983). *The Seven Laws of the Learner: How to Teach Almost Anything to Practically Anyone.* Multnomah Publishers Inc.

Wong, Harry and Rosemary, (1998). *The First Days of School.* Wong Publications.

Internet resources

Skills for each of the six levels of Bloom's Taxonomy [Counseling Services—University of Victoria]
www.coun.uvic.ca/learn/program/hndouts/bloom.html

MCQs and Bloom's Taxonomy [Cape Town, SA:UCT's page on Designing and Managing Multiple Choice Questions]
www.uct.ac.za/projects/cbe/mcqman/mcqappc.html

"The Last Day..."

By Jerry L. Parks

And so, it came to pass on the morning of the last day, that some beheld in the midst of their peers the noise of a fearsome and grievous tumult. Among the multitudes, amidst the howling and shutting of books, were seen those whose quest for knowledge lay scattered and broken upon the floor of opportunity. And from them was heard the sound of wailing and gnashing of teeth— yea, all hope was lost...and they were sore afraid. These were they who had left undone the things which they ought to have done, and had done not the things which they ought.

But lo, there were others—those who had been found abiding in their rooms keeping watch over their books by night. These were they upon whom obedient study had brought to plenitude much fruit. These arose in peace, for they had prepared themselves, and made straight the way of knowledge. Praise and adoration swelled in obeisance and rose in ebullient chorus to the gods of quiz and review! And these were called The Wise, but were known to some as 'The Burners of the Midnight Oil,' but to others as 'The Curve Wreckers.'

With lifted hands, and fingers callused by the purpose-ful etching of many notes upon their tablets, the cho-sen ones stepped forth, being anointed with the oil of gladness, and forever humbled by the merciful endow-ment of the great spirit known as extra credit. But for those who, in hubris, had straddled the line that lay betwixt the land of academic light and fooldom's chasm of great darkness—there was only silence, and their heart was heavy within them. The fate of the trembling multitudes was now left to be weighed upon the cold and impartial scales of mathematical formula, and their

FUTURE ADRIFT UPON THE TIMELESS OCEAN OF WAITING AS THE ELDERS GATHERED TOGETHER TO MARK THE TERMINAL EDICT KNOWN AS 'THE FINAL EXAM.'

AND, LO, MANY WOULD BE FOUND WANTING. THEY HAD COME TO PASS, BUT MANY TO PASS OUT...AND SOME NOT TO PASS AT ALL. AND THE MULTITUDE BEGAN TO REPENT OF THEIR WOEFUL HABITS OF STUDY, AND DREADED THEIR FATE. AT THE LAST, THERE WALKED AMONG THEM ONE KNOWN AS THE INSTRUCTOR, WHO TARRIED BUT A MOMENT. HE KNEW THAT MANY OF HIS TEACHINGS HAD FALLEN UPON FERTILE MINDS, WHILE OTHERS HAD FALLEN FLAT. HE TURNED FROM THEM SORROWFULLY, AND WENT UPON HIS WAY. AT THE LAST, AS SHADOWS LENGTHENED UPON THE LAST DAY, FATE DELIVERED ITS SENTENCE TO THE WAYWARD THRONGS. THE SILENCE OF THEIR SOLITUDE WAS BROKEN BY THE ANGUISHED TEARS OF RELIEF MOISTENING FURROWED BROWS, AS QUIVERING VOICES WERE HEARD TO PROCLAIM FROM THE VALLEY OF THE SHADOW OF DEATH: "...I SHALL NOT PASS THIS WAY AGAIN."

About the Author

Jerry Parks earned a B.S., M.A., & Ed.S. degrees in Education from Eastern Kentucky University, and completed additional graduate work at the University of Kentucky. He is a *National Board Certified Teacher*, and has received numerous "Teacher of the Year" honors at the local, state, and national level. He is a regular speaker at the *National Middle School Association* conferences, and is currently department chairman, and instructor of social studies at Georgetown Middle School in Georgetown, Kentucky.

Dr. Parks has two previously published books. "*With Joseph in the University of Adversity: The Mizraim Principles*", a study of the life of the Old Testament hero, Joseph, and guidelines for successful living based on the adversities he faced, and "*So, You Want to Become a National Board Certified Teacher?*" a handbook for teachers considering the National Board Certification Process.

Dr. Parks can be reached via e-mail at:
kidztchr7@hotmail.com or *jparks@scott.k12.ky.us.*

0-595-33094-0

7754121R0

Made in the USA
Lexington, KY
17 December 2010